LAST ACTS *of* KINDNESS

LAST ACTS *of* KINDNESS

LESSONS FOR THE LIVING FROM THE BEDSIDES OF THE DYING

Judith Redwing Keyssar

For my parents, Grace and Alex
My grandmother, Zipa Reise
My sister, Helene
All of my Friends who are on the "other side"
And for all the Beings who trusted me
to be present at their deathbeds

Out beyond
Ideas of wrongdoing
Or right-doing
There is a field.
I'll meet you there.

—*Rumi*

CONTENTS

Preface

FACING THE MIRROR OF MORTALITY

Everybody wants to go to Heaven, but nobody wants to die.
—*D. Nix*, from the song "Everybody Wants to Go to Heaven"

In the next twenty-five years the eighty million people born in the U.S. between 1946 and 1964 will demand that we face death differently. If the baby boomers are to change and reclaim death and dying in the same ways that they have changed the worldview of birth and living, they will require healthcare advocates in every field who understand and support this transformation. Healthcare professionals need a deeper understanding of what it means to serve people at the end of life and guide them through the mystery of death and dying, whether it be a physician working in the ICU, a nursing student experiencing clinical rounds for the first time, or a social worker trying to help a family in need. *Last Acts of Kindness* offers guidance through this delicate and challenging territory.

What is it about death and dying that scares us to such a degree that we avoid all conversation about it? What is it about this phase of life that creates such controversy among professionals? Why can't we understand that healing does not always mean living longer? What is this fierceness with which we do indeed rage against the darkness, the night, the unknown? If we are to answer any of these questions, we must begin the dialogue now—in private and in public, in our workplaces and our homes, with our patients, colleagues, families, and friends.

As children we wondered with curiosity, "What happened to Grandma?" Unknowingly, we contemplated great philosophical questions about life and death, how we got here, and where we go when we're gone. We were mesmerized by the vast darkness beyond the stars and wanted to know, "Where does the universe begin and end?" Children often do not fear death. As we get older and start to lose our friends and our families and sit at bedsides of patients or people we love, at some point we realize it will be our turn. And as quickly as this thought arises, we put it aside and admonish ourselves, "Oh, don't be silly. You're healthy. You're fine. Don't worry. Don't be morbid."

Death is not morbid. Life is the circle of breath that connects two precious moments in time: birth and death. Both are mysteries. My hope is that in sharing the stories and lessons of people whom I have attended in their dying process, a glimmer of light will be shed on what so many view as a topic of darkness. We can learn a great deal from each other, if we take the time to listen. We can learn what to expect in the dying process from those who have passed away and from those who stood vigil at their bedsides. Then perhaps we will not be so shocked or stunned when it is our time to serve the dying and witness this last act of life or to stand at the threshold ourselves. As healthcare professionals, our learning is never over. If one of these stories can influence the possibility of a more humane experience of dying, then this book has succeeded. Opening our hearts and minds means facing the mirror of our own mortality, with grace and compassion. This is not an easy task in a culture that denies impermanence, but it is a worthwhile practice, for those who are brave enough.

Death is the final taboo in our culture. We can talk about illness and religion, politics and sex, gender and race issues, but the *D* word is still difficult for people to utter in polite company. The advent of palliative care and the constantly increasing use of hospice services in this country have begun to change this, but we still have a long way to go. The baby boomers have worked hard to reclaim rituals and rites of passages surrounding birth and other life transitions. Let us now empower this generation and those to come by encouraging honest conversations and allowing ourselves to design our lives with the understanding that death is not merely a medical event. Let us change the face of dying in our culture from one of fear and anxiety to one of acceptance and compassion. Inevitable as death is for all beings, let us work to create experiences that are positive, potent, and transformational.

NOTE: The names of the people and some of the details of these stories have been altered to protect confidentiality. Some personal reflections and observations accompany the stories.

Prologue

MIDWIFE TO THE DYING

We are not human beings having a spiritual experience.
We are spiritual beings having a human experience.

—*Teilhard de Chardin*, French theologian

The dark train slowly wound its way out of the forest, grey smoke pouring out of the smokestack. Zipa stood transfixed, wondering how this huge vehicle could be coming toward her without horses. It was a miracle! The year was 1887, and it was the first train to come through Staraconstantinov, her tiny Russian village.

In 1969, this same woman, now my ninety-two-year-old grandmother, sat transfixed in front of a television as she watched the first men land on the moon. "Is this a miracle?" she wondered out loud. Zipa Reise Keyssar lived through five wars, resided in five countries, and spoke five languages. A fierce and determined youngest child and the only girl in an orthodox Jewish family, she insisted on being educated. In order to attend school and get a job, she had to leave her village home and travel to Kiev. She became a nurse and a midwife. Zipa survived her husband's suicide, her relatives' extermination by the Nazis, and nursed her dying daughter while bombs were falling around her in London during World War II. When she finally landed in America, she couldn't know what a powerful influence she would have on her granddaughter, many years later.

The life of a Russian immigrant was one of adversity, as were the lives of so many in the early part of the twentieth century. It was a welcome moment when, on a cold and wintry night, January 19, 1971, in a small, rural village in northern Vermont, Zipa died in her sleep—the kind of peaceful death that so many of us hope for. This, indeed, was a miracle.

Zipa died the day before my eighteenth birthday. She had been my teacher and role model, and somehow it did not feel like coincidence that her death collided with my birth. I felt more honored than sad, and in that moment, I realized something profound about the relationship of life to death, and the miracle of each one. I understood that life is a circle, a spiral, not a linear continuum with a clear beginning and solid end. I felt a strong sense, deep in my heart and mind, that whatever we understand as "spirit" goes on. I knew then that this knowledge would shape my life.

❧

Years later and on the other edge of the continent, on September 8, 1988, the telephone rang just as I arrived home from work. The house was dark and cold, and I was ready to build a fire and start making dinner. One of my land partners had just come in, too, and we both looked at the phone not wanting to answer it. I knew intuitively, however, the moment I heard it ring, what this call was about. I picked up the phone and heard the voice of a strange man asking if I was Judith Keyssar and did I know a Kate M.?

"Yes, of course," I answered, sensing that he was going to try to tell me, in a considerate way, that there had been a serious accident.

"Do you know where her family is and how I can contact them?" he asked.

"Yes, yes, I do, but her family is far away in New Jersey, and I am, well, I'm her closest friend here, and you could consider me *family* too, so please tell me what has happened."

According to legal protocol, he could not give me details, but he managed to let me know that she had been in a motorcycle accident and was in critical condition in the Intensive Care Unit at Marin General Hospital. Marin General was about a three-hour drive from where I lived, in California's Mendocino County. I hung up and called the hospital immediately, and again, because I was not a blood relative, they could not reveal details. Thankfully, the compassionate nurse on the other end of the line was able to understand the situation and tell me that if I wanted to see Kate alive, I had better come quickly.

My life took a drastic turn that night. I drove through the dark corridor of redwoods along the winding river road to the freeway and arrived at the hospital where I would spend the next three weeks, waiting for signs of life. My life transformed during that time, in ways that I would only fully understand much later.

The initial shock was the most difficult part. Kate was a strong, thin young woman with a full head of black curls and penetrating brown eyes. Since she enjoyed costumes and flamboyant clothes, she had no problem wearing the leather jacket and pants recommended for motorcycle drivers. But the helmet—no—that offended her sense of freedom. So, when I walked into the room, arriving at her feet first and then slowly inching along beside her thin legs that were unscathed, her torso intact, and even her arms barely scratched, it was hard not to gasp at the sight of her head, which was at least four times its normal size and looked like a large black-and-blue balloon. She looked like some bizarre science fiction creature, with tubes in every orifice and electrical wires and IV lines connected to pumps and monitors, each with its own noise and alarm system. If I had not recognized her body from the shoulders down, I would certainly not have known this person.

"Kate," I tried to speak her name calmly, believing, as the nurse had said, that she still might be able to hear me. "I'm here. Robin and Nancy are here, too. We will be with you. Everyone loves you and is sending prayers. I called your parents; they will be here tomorrow with your sisters."

> It is a completely unrealistic expectation to think that people who have never seen someone in critical condition in a hospital are going to know how to act and know what is appropriate. I wanted to scream and cry and lie down on the bed and hold her, but her bed constantly rotated from side to side and up to down, like a strange ride in an amusement park. No one encouraged me to touch her or make human contact. It seemed that whenever anyone came in, it was to do a "job" and not to offer comfort. It was frightening.

Kate had a large circle of friends, and we set up camp in the ICU waiting room. We had our sleeping bags and food, and surprisingly, we were not asked to leave. When her family arrived, they reserved motel rooms nearby, and we rotated going there for showers and naps. We instinctively understood that, regardless of what would happen, Kate needed to be surrounded by loving energy and people who knew and understood her.

Each night after eleven o'clock, when the last shift of nurses settled in and the hustle and bustle of the hospital calmed, I would slip into the ICU and sit at Kate's bedside—singing, praying, and simply being a healing presence. I didn't know if she would live or die. I had never seen anyone on life support before, and it was terrifying and awkward. I would have conversations with Kate, believing she was responding with a squeeze of the hand or the blink of her eye. I had faith that she felt me at her bedside. I asked Kate to let me know what she wanted to do—to let go of this life or try to return, under-standing that life as she knew it would never be the same. I held her hand, touched her heart, and tried to feel whatever life force was left in this beautiful young woman.

Days crawled by and nothing seemed to change. Some days Kate would squeeze someone's hand tightly, and immediately we all would hope it meant that her brain was functioning again, but this did not seem to be the case. Finally, I went to the neurosurgeon and asked, "Dr. Abrams, if this was your best friend, what would you do? Would you take her off life support?" I liked and respected her doctor. He was kind and soft-spoken, and never seemed to be in a hurry to get somewhere else. He actually sat down with me and said, "I have seen many people in this state, after traumatic accidents with no hope for recovery. You just don't ever know who will survive. Your friend is young and strong, and her vital organs are still functioning even though the damage to her brain is extensive. This is the kind of case where we must wait and see what God has planned. "

I listened to this gentle man. I understood that we must all be patient and sit with our not knowing. Deep inside, I also knew that it would actually be a blessing if Kate were to let go, because I sensed that she would never recover fully.

Each time I walked through the steel doors of the ICU, I felt that I was hearing a clear voice, not unlike my grandmother's, telling me that my true work in this life was to become a midwife to the dying—a title I had never heard used before, although it has become a more common term since then.

The next night when I went to her bedside, I felt a change: Kate was less aware, farther away. I felt myself begin to cry, and a flood of tears rushed down as I held her hand and told her it was okay if she needed to leave us. After the deluge, I felt a release and a feeling of serenity. I told Kate of the voice I kept hearing, telling me that I was meant to be a nurse and that I knew now that my work in the world was about being with people who were dying. I felt directed to be a midwife to spirits waiting to cross over. I took her hand, kissed it gently, and thanked her for giving me this amazing and powerful gift.

We celebrated Kate's thirtieth birthday with a ritual on the lawn of the hospital. Friends from all over California, along with her family from the East Coast, gathered to celebrate her life. A week later, Kate developed complications from pneumonia. As she was being wheeled back from a routine x-ray, she "coded," as it is euphemistically called. Her heart had stopped, and the hospital staff immediately began pumping on her chest, calling for the electric paddles, to try to resuscitate her. After many attempts, her family finally said, "Please stop. God has made the decision."

✍

I had been my father's last hope for a doctor in the family to follow in his footsteps. Although my mother did not voice it until later, she secretly wished I would become a nurse, following in her footsteps instead. However, as a young adult, rebelling against establishment ideas, I dropped out of my pre-med academic track and avoided western medicine like the plague. It was the 1970s, and the world was wild and enticing, beckoning to be explored, and I could not commit to late nights in university libraries studying biochemistry and physics. I left the Ivy Leagues and headed to California, to become an artist and activist, to learn from teachers of various spiritual traditions, and to understand my own inner workings of heart and soul. I found my voice as a songwriter and my power as a public speaker and leader of community ceremonies.

Life has a way of teaching us its lessons, and love brings us home to our hearts. Throughout the years of finding my path—through art and music and writing, by living on land in rural settings, through studying nutrition and bodywork, meditation practices and rituals of healing—I saw more and more clearly that my heart's work was about service and healing.

I began nursing school the month after Kate died, knowing that in order to attend people who were dying, there was much to learn. This was the gift that Kate gave me. I became an RN as quickly as I could and began working in hospitals, then became certified in oncology and eventually found my niche as the charge nurse of an intensive care unit.

The next turning point in my professional life occurred after several years of working in intensive care with people who were critically ill, many of whom were dying and many of whom were on life support. I witnessed too many people in hospitals dying alone and afraid, without adequate pain management, and with their friends and families confused and distraught. I heard countless unsatisfactory conversations between healthcare professionals and families, in which the reluctance to tell the truth about a patient's condition was a major stumbling block. Although I did work in a small, rural hospital with a much more user-friendly intensive care unit than most large urban hospitals have, I still witnessed one too many difficult and prolonged endings of lives, mainly because important and candid conversations that needed to happen in a timely manner did not.

Toward the end of my time working in ICU, I attended two seminars that redirected me, personally and professionally. The first was a one-day workshop taught by Angeles Arrien, titled *Creativity and Generativity in the Second Half of Life*. The workshop requested us to look at the gifts and talents we acquired during the first half of our lives and utilize them by giving back to the world, in whatever ways we could, during the second half. I knew that one of my gifts was my emotional ease with death and dying supported by my medical knowledge, understanding, and intuition. Another gift was my experience with rituals, music, art and complementary healing modalities, which would prove to be crucial to the practice of holistic nursing.

The other seminar I attended was with Joan Halifax, a medical anthropologist and Buddhist teacher. She conducts a ten-day course for healthcare professionals called *Being with Dying*. These two courses changed my life. They opened me to deeper understanding of my own mortality and helped me integrate that knowledge into my clinical practice and my own teaching. I have come to deeply appreciate Joan Halifax's translation of a passage from Rilke: *Love and death are the great gifts that are given to us. Mostly they are passed on unopened.*

❧

Twenty years later, I continue to feel blessed by the gifts of love and death that I am regaled with constantly. Even so, my early experiences were not always easy. In most nursing and medical school programs, very little is taught about how to deal with dying patients. The *messiness* of birth and death is not highlighted, either. I remember one morning, as a student nurse, walking into the room of a man who was actively dying. I was stunned by the chaos in the room, the secretions coming from his wide-open mouth, and the sickening smell in the air. I was not prepared for some of the physical realities of the last moments of life, nor was I prepared emotionally for the helplessness and lack of control that I experienced. After the patient died, my nursing instructor told me to shave him and clean him up for his family. I followed these orders, and then in my charting of the day, I wrote a poetic comment as my way of dealing with the emotions. I was reprimanded and reminded that a chart is a legal document and not a term paper. Fortunately, this did not dissuade me from my nursing career or from my goal of becoming a midwife to the dying.

❧

During childbirth, we hover over the mother's bed as she yells and groans in pain and pushes and tightens and pants. We hold her hands and rub her back. Sometimes we administer strong drugs, and other times we allow nature to take her course. There are fluids—blood, sweat and tears and more. Sometimes it happens quickly, and other times it takes days. And we wait. We wait for this miracle—for a tiny human being to emerge from the waters and the darkness, after a challenging journey through a tight tunnel. And then, being blinded by a great light, the baby screams and takes his or her first breath. Life! We greet this new person with celebration and profound love and joy. We are ecstatic to witness what can only be described as a spiritual experience. We understand that first breath as an awakening, and we welcome a spirit to this earth, embodied as a fragile human being.

Witnessing a death is also an incredible honor, each one unique in its form, enriching in its lessons, poignant in its depth. Here, too, we hover over the bedside, try to ease the suffering and pain, and allow the body and soul to do their final dance so that the spirit can be released to what many hope and believe is a great light, a luminous and loving God, or an infinite and welcoming spaciousness. I continue to learn from each person I attend and from each family member and friend who stands beside a person they love. I have watched people change drastically and open to life in new and unexpected ways, after being at the bedside of a loved one. The simplest and most profound lesson that I have learned over and over again is that love is truly all that matters, and in the end, a force much greater than our small human lives connects us all.

When you were born, you cried, and the world rejoiced.
Live your life so that when you die,
The world cries and you rejoice.

—*Native American saying*

Part One

DEATH: MEDICAL EVENT
OR SPIRITUAL EXPERIENCE?

STORIES OF PEOPLE WHO DIED IN HOSPITALS

Medicine as chemistry alone is the
materialized longing for things to be otherwise.

—Anonymous

The stories in this section are about people who died in hospitals. Some of them knew they were dying, others died unexpectedly. Some had been suffering with long and involved illnesses, while others came into the emergency room or intensive care unit in crisis. These are some of the many ways that people die in our society. As professionals in the healthcare system, the more knowledge, understanding and compassion that we have about the dying process, the less we will be consumed by fear or intimidated by a system that prides itself on saving lives. We must learn when to set aside our clinical expertise and technical ability and take the time to consider the most appropriate action for someone who is about to die.

In many cases, our ability to save a life is a blessing. People who have had traumatic accidents or a surgical complication or even serious pneumonia can be maintained on mechanical ventilation and chemical support in order to get them through a crisis. Even when people have advance directives that state they would not want to be kept alive on machines, there are various reasons and times when it feels most appropriate in the moment to try to sustain life. During my years working in ICU, I witnessed dozens of people whom we thought would never survive walk out of the hospital. The healing of serious illness or trauma often felt miraculous.

However, when someone is clearly dying and on what we call life support, it can create many layers of confusion for loved ones as well as for healthcare practitioners. Once we have gone through all the procedures required to put someone on life support, deciding to take them off is not as easy a task. Doctors and nurses often feel the burden of having to prove to families why their loved one will not survive. Family members and healthcare professionals alike are plagued by the concept of pulling the plug, believing that they will then be responsible for someone's death.

The words *life support* conjure up distinct images in this day and age. We see it on television and in the movies—busy hospital rooms filled with people in uniforms rushing around with syringes and computer monitors and wires everywhere. A person lies in a bed, connected to machines and IV drips, and the chest rises and falls. The person appears to be alive.

This concept of life support is an outgrowth of modern medical science and technology. We have the capability to keep people alive, often indefinitely, and always at great cost. We can put a dead person's heart into a living person, give someone new kidneys or lungs, and even transplant the very marrow of a person's bones. We can resuscitate people and bring them back to life after they have died by breathing for them and sending electrical shocks to the muscles of the heart, which restarts the impulses between cells and creates the current so vital to life.

And why do we do these things? Because we can. We live in a society that will not look directly into the mirror of mortality without squirming or quickly turning away. The media want us to believe that people can and should live forever—or at least longer than their bodies are willing or able to. Commercials and advertisements flood us with images and information about how to stay young, look young, and avoid the aging process—insinuating that if we don't age, perhaps we won't have to die.

🖎

In the United States, most people still die in hospitals. Part of reclaiming our power in caring for those at the end of life lies in learning how to be advocates. We must be willing to speak the truth and ask for what is needed or desired, whether we are a professional, a family member or a friend. The designated agent on an advance directive—durable power of attorney for healthcare carries the responsibility and obligation to speak for the person who cannot. If the agent believes that the patient would not want a particular procedure or treatment, like a feeding tube or antibiotics, the agent has the right and the duty to speak up. The healthcare professionals have the duty to listen.

The advent of hospital-based palliative care services is increasing both professional and public awareness about what it means to offer compassion, respect and comfort for patients and their families, whether it is behind the curtains of a busy ICU, in a special palliative care suite, or in a regular hospital bed. Palliative care is about easing suffering—physical, emotional and spiritual. We can ease suffering in any venue. Those who understand the realm of palliative care must be willing to help educate those who do not. Doctors and nurses need to expand their view of palliative care in order to appropriately serve their patients. Patients and families need to know how to access a palliative care team before their loved one is in crisis.

🖎

Death is not a medical event. It is indeed a spiritual experience. So often in hospitals, there are loud noises, machines, and constantly ringing alarms. Visitors feel separated from loved ones by bedrails and IV lines and often feel too intimidated by the aura of authority to unlatch the rail and simply sit on the bed or touch the person who is lying there. Sometimes, touch can be the most healing treatment we have to offer.

Just because a person is dying in a hospital does not mean that death is less sacred than if they were dying at home in a more natural environment. Hospital chaplains are allies when it comes to working with the nursing and medical staff to ensure that people have needed time with loved ones for emotions, for rituals, for clergy, before or after the death occurs, or both. They can often direct family to a quiet space in which to discuss the spiritual needs of the patient or conduct a simple ceremony. I believe that it should be protocol to ensure that the patient's and family's wishes are honored throughout the process of dying and death. More importantly, those who are experienced and skilled in the "art" of medicine need to help empower patients and their loved ones to ask for what they need in order to create a safe and sacred environment.

๛

Life is the lesson. Love is the teacher.

—*Chante Edison*

The suffering of the dying cannot always be subdued with anti-anxiety agents or painkillers. We do not always know the cause of a patient's emotional or spiritual suffering, but often we can sense it. When a good friend of mine was near the end of her life and her body was riddled with metastatic cancer, she was on many different medications to keep her comfortable. The most significant pain she described to me, however, was her feeling of betrayal by her husband. She would cry for hours, but this type of pain was not some-thing that any amount of Vicodin or morphine could alleviate. It is love and compassion that soothe these wounds.

Yet I have also witnessed that love can hold people back from their final journeys. Sometimes when people are surrounded by a group of loving friends and family, it is harder for them to let go of this earthly plane and detach the last thread that holds their spirit to the body. It is indeed a common occurrence that at the moment all of the family and friends finally leave the room, the person dies. For some, it is important to be holding a hand and for others it is important to leave this world alone. Every human is unique, and the stories of our deaths are as individual and poignant as the stories of our births and of our lives.

❧

QUESTIONS TO CONSIDER

As you read the stories in this book, imagine yourself in the scenario as best you can. Some situations may upset you, while others will resonate deeply. I ask you now, as you begin to read, to please sit with the feelings and ideas that arise. Then ask yourself, if you were in the dying process, what would be most important for you? Please consider, as a healthcare professional and as a human being sharing this planet with so many others, if you have never truly pondered the great questions of life and death for yourself, how are you going to be of service to those who reach the end of the journey before you?

Some questions to consider as you read these stories:

- How would your feelings change if you were the doctor, nurse, social worker, chaplain, family member, or patient?

- What would be the most challenging part of any given scenario? The place? The decisions to be made? The necessary communications?

- What would you do differently?

- Which person in the story do you feel the most affinity for or aversion to? How would you communicate with that person?

- What are the psychological, emotional, and/or spiritual challenges in the scenario?

- What would you need to learn, do, or understand in order to create what you would consider to be a positive outcome?

- How would you take care of yourself in the situation?

- What lessons have you learned from these stories?

- What has touched your heart when you have experienced a death?

PULLING THE PLUG

Suzanne takes you down to her place by the river.
—*Leonard Cohen*, from the song "Suzanne"

S uzy was a fiery redhead in her fifties—a bright spot in any crowd or in any hospital. She was always positive and spoke her mind, even when she was bald and sick from chemotherapy. Her shining eyes and smile beckoned, even in the darkest of times. I was drawn to Suzy by her spunk, humor and keen senses of both style and observation. In nursing school, I was cautioned not to befriend patients or their families. There have been times in my career when the human, heartfelt connection was so strong that this rule was impossible to follow. This was one of those times.

I was Suzy's oncology nurse over a long period of time and administered chemotherapy for her esophageal cancer. When you spend this kind of time with a person, you hear their stories and learn their fears. You witness their relationships and see how they are connected to their loved ones. Suzy and Martin had been married for many years, their children grown and gone, and their love and passion still palpable and strong. Martin would spend long hours at the hospital during Suzy's chemo treatments. When the final treatment was completed, Suzy and Martin felt relief and joy.

The relief lasted for a brief time.

Less than a year later, Suzy was transported back to the hospital via ambulance, due to a serious bowel obstruction. After years of suffering and then finally reclaiming a normal life, it was tragic to hear the news that now Suzy had colon cancer.

> In the past, I used the concept of a roller-coaster ride to describe the drastic ups and downs of life, particularly with chronic illness. Recently I have come to the conclusion that "riding the waves" better illustrates this phenomenon. Floating over ocean waves can be less frightening and nauseating than riding a roller coaster, and most of us have experienced being tossed or held down by a wave and surviving. Cancer patients go through months and years of symptoms, diagnoses, emotional/physical reactions, treatments of all kinds, more illness, and then, potentially, freedom from disease. For some, this freedom, which we call remission, lasts a long time and deserves celebration. For others, however, remission is short-lived, and malignant cells appear in another place in the body. Either way, nagging questions and fears torment cancer survivors every day: Will it return? When? Where? What will happen next? Will I be offered more treatment? Will I die? How do I retain hope?

Suzy's cancer returned with a vengeance. Her intestinal blockages were cleared and she left the hospital—only to return a week later. After major surgery, she was admitted to the ICU, where her post-op prognosis was poor. Her body was too weak to continue fighting and most likely too compromised to heal after surgery. She was put on full life support, which included a ventilator and IV medications. Thankfully for Suzy, she was medicated and sedated and did not feel much pain. For Martin, the suffering was intolerable.

This is often a difficult time for healthcare professionals, because we understand that in the case of a terminal illness, life support only prolongs the quantity of life and not the quality. However, for family and friends of the patient, this can be an important time. A few extra days or a week to process feelings surrounding a loved one's death can help to ease the grief and the letting go. We all come to acceptance and closure differently, and this part of the dying and grieving process must be honored.

If you have never witnessed life support in the ER or ICU, it would be an educational experience to see someone in this condition and to imagine yourself as the person in the bed. Patients appear to be untouchable because of all the tubes and wires and machines. However, often what people in this state need the most is the touch and sound of someone they love, and it is important for healthcare professionals to facilitate this as much as they can.

Martin was deeply in love with Suzy. Each time he entered the ICU, tears formed in his eyes. Martin understood that Suzy was dying. Regardless, he would shake his head and announce that he could not imagine pulling the plug.

One day a chaplain came into the ICU to visit with Suzy and Martin. After his prayers for Suzy, he offered to take a walk outside with Martin. When they returned Martin's eyes revealed that a release of tears had occurred, and he seemed clearly changed. We hugged and I asked him about his talk with the chaplain.

Martin said, "He helped me understand that this is not about my pulling the plug. It's not like I am going to bring about Suzy's death by taking her off the ventilator. I finally understood that stopping the ventilator is about allowing God to make the final decision and allowing nature to take its course. Taking Suzy off the ventilator isn't about relinquishing hope; it's about relinquishing the false assumption that *we* are in control here. I don't want to let Suzy die, but her fate is not up to me. I need to allow her spirit to be free. I really get it now."

Words will never make the dying process an easy one, but the right conversation at the right time can help the surrender to the inevitable with added trust and confidence. I put my arm around Martin and we stood quietly in Suzy's presence for what seemed like an eternity. When I reached to turn off one of the alarms on the IV machine, Martin said, "Please call whomever you need to. It's time to let her go."

Suzy's doctor arrived shortly thereafter. Martin chose not to be present for the physical disconnection from the ventilator. For many, this act is too difficult to watch. Believing in the common wisdom that hearing is the last sense to go, as I turned off the machine and the tube was taken out of Suzy's throat, I whispered to her, "Martin and your daughters love you *so* much." Suzy did not linger, as some do when they are extubated. Her life story ended as soon as mechanical ventilation stopped.

When the team completed the technological duties, I called Martin back into the ICU. He could not hide his tears any longer. He wept in honor of the end of his life with Suzy and the end of her suffering. I wept as well; Martin and Suzy had become dear friends, despite any protocol or caution.

A few months after Suzy's passing, Martin visited the ICU. It was important to him to thank the nurses and doctors and share his feelings of loss. We spend such intimate time with families of patients in the dying process, and then suddenly the relationship ends. Martin expressed that what he appreciated most was the space we allowed, to be real, to be honest, to be afraid. We had given him the freedom and time to integrate the harsh reality and his overwhelmingly sad feelings. Martin recognized this as a gift.

Often in hospitals, the "us against them" stigma exists—those with knowledge, expertise and information versus those who are sick or dying or fragile and exhausted from attending a loved one in an unfamiliar environment. Many nurses and doctors are skilled clinicians but are not comfortable with death and the human, emotional process surrounding it. Until recently, most have not had serious training dealing with death and dying. In addition, the success of professional achievements is often measured by the medical aspects of saving lives. Doctors and nurses can experience a sense of failure when a patient dies in the hospital.

As a nurse, I am involved with death on a regular basis. It is a delicate balance for us healthcare professionals to maintain emotional distance while offering comfort and competence. We must consciously keep our hearts open to the fragile people all around us. It is important to remember that a hospital healthcare team is composed of human beings who have also lost loved ones and suffer in their own ways, even if they do not reveal that side of their personalities. I like to remember the words of Dr. Rachel Naomi Remen (1997, Riverhead), from her book, *Kitchen Table Wisdom*: "The healing of suffering is compassion, not expertise."

THIRD-DEGREE HEART BLOCK

Listen, listen, listen to my heart song.
I will never forget you, I will never forsake you,
I will always remember, I will always be with you.

—*Paramahansa Yogananda*

The heart is a powerful force—on many levels. All blood within the body filters through the heart, sustaining each and every cell structure and organ in our bodies. The heart is a complex system of electrical impulses and mechanical and muscular contractures that are based on the interplay of electrolytes: calcium, magnesium, potassium, and sodium. Hearts can become blocked in many different ways. In medicine, we primarily consider first, second, and third degrees of heart block. These blockages refer to various problems with the electrical conductivity of the cells in the heart muscle. Third-degree heart block is the most serious.

Healing does not always result in living. Margaret was ninety-four years old. She was admitted to the ICU after suffering a massive heart attack, and we were having trouble converting her third-degree heart block back to a normal rhythm. She also had a gangrenous gall bladder, which could not be operated on due to the heart attack. By all logic, it was time for Margaret to let go, but here she remained, in the ICU.

A normal protocol of drugs was administered: atropine, dopamine, and others, as well as morphine for her pain. She would awaken briefly, shout out in hallucination, and then fade back into the pillows. Each time she faded, we thought she might die, yet she would continually return for another round, much to our surprise. Her heart was so weak and fragile.

Margaret had been in the ICU for a week, and transitioned in and out of consciousness. On a Monday night, I asked her, "Do you understand what is happening to you?"

"Not really," she replied in her sleepy but alert voice. I tried to explain, in simple terms, what was happening with her heart and infected gall bladder. She looked at me with soft eyes and said, "I feel like I almost died a couple of times."

"You did," I told her bluntly. Taking this opportunity to stay and probe a bit deeper, I asked, "Were you afraid?"

Margaret's voice got very quiet and tears ran down her thin pale cheeks. "Oh, no, honey, I'm not afraid of dying. It would be such a welcome relief. It would be fine to die right now…and honey, thank you for talking to me about it. Everyone seems so afraid to tell me that I'm dying."

I left work the next morning, after a twelve-hour night shift, feeling sad yet fulfilled. I knew that I would not see Margaret again, and at the same time, I felt pleased that we had spoken. Western medicine has a myriad of protocols for blocked hearts, but they don't always work, especially in the frail elderly. When there is nothing more we can do to heal the heart, the greatest healing we can offer is our compassion and honesty. As healthcare professionals, we must let go of our fears of failing and our inability to fix everything, in order to be present for a patient's last conscious moments. Perhaps in this way, we do actually return the flow of energy to a blocked heart so that it can stop in peace.

LISTENING FROM THE HEART:
THE ROLE OF THE ADVOCATE

I have seen that the prognosis may not be the reality any more than the map is the territory or the blueprint, the building.

—*Dr. Rachel Naomi Remen, Kitchen Table Wisdom,* 1997

As one of the few certified oncology nurses in a small hospital, other nurses often asked me to explain a doctor's cancer diagnosis and treatment plan to patients and families. One such day, Carol, the nurse on the medical floor, came to the ICU asking me to speak with a man and his wife about his late-stage pancreatic cancer and the plan to start chemotherapy immediately.

Kevin was in his mid-forties. He and his wife Juliette had moved to the community only recently. Thus, they had few friends and no connection to the medical establishment. Only one oncologist practiced in this small town at the time. This is one of the challenges of living in a beautiful, rural place, far from high-tech medicine and second opinions.

Kevin and Juliette wanted to know what their options were, if any. They had many questions: Must Kevin undergo chemotherapy? Must he really start right away? He had rarely been to a doctor or even been sick until recently, when he began experiencing vague but painful abdominal symptoms. Kevin was hesitant to start down the treacherous path of Western medical treatment with its notorious side effects. He did know enough about chemotherapy from friends who had cancer to be wary of it. Kevin had thus far only trusted alternative or complementary medicine. When I told Kevin and Juliette that they did not need to make a decision immediately, they were relieved.

Cancer takes a long time to grow within the body. Fortunately and unfortunately, it often does not cause a lot of pain or symptoms until late in its course. Pancreatic cancer often seems to present itself too late for most people to have much quality time left. There are always exceptions of course, but Kevin was not an exception. After going home and sitting with his options for a few days, Kevin decided he was more at ease with the idea of dying than undergoing chemotherapy.

> Patients with cancer have the right to choose their path. There are some oncologists who firmly believe that treatment should begin as soon as a diagnosis is confirmed, and others are willing to give patients time to consider their options. For someone with advanced pancreatic cancer (or other late-stage or metastatic disease), it may be questionable if chemotherapy would make a difference in longevity or mortality, or even in relief of symptoms. In many cases, the treatments for cancer cause more suffering than the actual disease. Cancer patients must be given all of the information available in order to make clear decisions about a plan that will have huge consequences on the quality of their lives. Many are told that chemotherapy is their only option. That is simply not true.

Providing comfort and healing involves more than taking vital signs, recording patient histories, listening to heart and lung sounds, and reading lab tests and scans. Healing takes time. It requires learning about a patient holistically. The complexities of a life and personality must be understood. Healing requires time spent with the sick patient in order to grasp the issues beyond a particular disease. Unfortunately, in present-day healthcare, practitioners do not have the time to get to know their patients, let alone sit with them through a complicated decision-making process. Many doctors tend to see a cancer diagnosis, and because their number-one responsibility is to try to cure disease and save lives, they assume that a patient will agree to any treatment offered. It is also assumed most people want to live at any cost.

Kevin and Juliette were willing to confront death head-on, rather than suffer through treatment and lose any remaining quality of life. Kevin went home for a few weeks but ended up back in the hospital because his pain was so severe that it could not be managed at home. This happens. Home hospice teams are not always able to manage certain severe levels of pain that require IV medications. Kevin spent his last week of life in the hospital, with Juliette snuggled next to him in his small hospital bed. Some hospitals are able to provide private rooms for the dying. Kevin and Juliette decorated his room and hung pictures and objects of art and spirit that were meaningful to them. The staff loved entering Kevin's room because there was a sense of peace and calm. There was no urgency. His pain was managed, and he and Juliette simply soaked up every last minute of their lives together.

It is a blessing for healthcare staff to witness this level of comfort with death. It teaches us to slow down and accept the reality surrounding death in ways that we are not taught in nursing or medical school.

As a nurse, one of my key jobs is to serve as an advocate for patients. When I encounter situations where it is clear that a doctor or medical team is not listening to the patient's feelings or wishes, it is difficult and frustrating. Difficult because it means confronting doctors about their communication styles and about their own fears. Frustrating because as a nurse, I sometimes do not feel heard by the doctors, either. It is so crucial that we see each other as members of a healthcare *team* and respect our different levels of understanding and expertise.

While I was attending to Kevin and Juliette, another patient and well-regarded community member, June, was undergoing treatment for metastatic lung cancer. Regardless of over a year of chemotherapy and radiation, the cancer continued to spread. In July, during her last hospitalization, she was feeling terrible. Her pain was difficult to manage, and she was expressing to everyone that she felt she was dying. One of her doctors walked into her room and said, "Oh, don't worry, June, you'll get through this. I expect a Christmas card from you." After the doctor left the room, June sat up in bed, red-faced and angry, and with all the energy she could muster, said to her family, "Who the hell does she think she is, telling me she expects a Christmas card. We ALL know I'll be dead long before that." June died two weeks later.

Recently, a friend of mine, who had been a hospice patient for many months and was close to her death, told the story of her experience with chemotherapy. She said that when she was diagnosed with breast cancer, she realized that even though she was a "healer" herself and a strong believer in alternative medicines, she needed to experience what Western medicine had to offer. Her doctor let her know that she was getting the "Cadillac" of treatment protocols, and he expected a full remission of her disease. After several months of feeling devastated by the chemotherapy, Cathy decided to stop the Western treatments. Her doctor was shocked and offered a different protocol of drugs that he thought might not make her as sick. Cathy reported looking at him quizzically and saying, "But Doctor, if I didn't want the Cadillac, why would I opt for a Volkswagen?"

It is going to take doctors, nurses, lawyers, and consumer advocates (patients) to help change the healthcare system in the U.S. Each time you hear of a friend or loved one in a hospital, it is important to show up. It is crucial that the healthcare team attending to them is actually listening and paying attention to the patient's needs. The patient must not be made to feel inferior because they have an illness. It is our duty, not just as professionals but as human beings who care for one another, to insist that *healing* be put back into the language of healthcare. There are many definitions of healing. Jeanne Achterberg, PhD, author, lecturer and patient advocate, in her book *Woman as Healer* (1991), offers us these:

- Healing is a lifelong journey toward wholeness.

- Healing is remembering what has been forgotten about connection, and unity and interdependence among all things living and nonliving.

- Healing is embracing what is most feared.

- Healing is opening what has been closed, softening what hardened into obstruction.

- Healing is entering into the transcendent, timeless moment when one experiences the divine.

- Healing is creativity and passion and love.

- Healing is seeking and expressing self in its fullness, its light and shadow, its male and female.

- Healing is learning to trust life.

And I believe that healing is also learning to accept that death is part of life.

WHEN THE INTERVENTION
IS HOLDING A HAND

I wanna die easy, when I die.

—*Traditional song*

At five in the morning, I walked down the long, semi-dark corridor of the medical-surgical ward of a city hospital. For days, Mr. Perry had been in bed, barely responsive, his breathing rapid and shallow. His skin was a deep yellow, and his body exuded a strong odor that did not subside after the cursory morning sponge bath that he received from a nursing assistant. He had no family, and his friends did not come to visit anymore.

I walked into his room in the dim lamplight and sensed Mr. Perry's spirit hovering close to his body but almost disconnected. I dusted the air around him with a gesture of sweeping away any bad spirits or dreams. Then I gently took one of his hands in mine and put my other hand on his heart—a gesture that a person in bed often seems to find soothing. It comforts me as well. "Mr. Perry, it's Redwing," I whispered, "I'm holding your hand. You're still in the hospital." After a few moments of silence and a quick assessment of his breathing and heart rate, I said softly, "It's OK to go now, if you are ready. There will be hands to hold on the other side.

It's OK to let go, Mr. Perry." I began to sing to him in a low, quiet voice. His eyes opened for a moment and he started moaning, softly. "Mama, mama," were the first words he had uttered in days. Somewhere deep inside this man's heart and struggling-to-let-go spirit, it seemed that a connection had been made. He responded with the first word that most of us utter.

A half hour later, I walked into the room again as I made my final rounds of the morning. Another nurse walked by the door and asked, "Did Mr. Perry die yet?" I smiled as I looked around the curtain at his finally serene face. The fast and labored breathing had ended, and what remained was a calm expression on his wrinkleless face. "Yes," I said out loud. "Mr. Perry has gone."

> The human spirit gasps for breath and grasps for life for as long as it possibly can. There is a tenacity with which we hold onto these last precious moments, to all the elements that we are losing hold of—earth, air, fire, and water—even when we are alone and in pain.

> What a blessing to imagine that we could be held in some tender way and that our suffering may be relieved, even if we are alone in a hospital. This sentiment seems so basic, and yet it is still a lot to expect of our culture. So many health-care professionals remain fearful of death and try to avoid it. I've heard many nurses say, "I'm glad he (or she) didn't die on my shift."

> Since dying in hospitals is still so common in our culture, we must educate hospital staff about compassionate care for each and every dying patient. We must encourage the understanding that the last breaths are as holy as the first ones, and it is an honor to witness them, not a curse.

DANNY BOY

Oh Danny boy, the pipes, the pipes are calling.
—*F. Weatherly*, from the song "Danny Boy"

Danny was a gentleman farmer—a sweet and kind gay man who loved the earth. Danny always came to the annual Ladies Lawn and Garden Party dressed in perfect Southern belle drag. Tall, thin and good-looking, Danny was quiet and elegant. And his voice—oh my, the voice of an angel. He sang in the local choirs, and crowds flocked to church to hear Danny perform a solo.

No one imagined that Danny would die of AIDS. Even when all of his friends were dying, somehow Danny would be immune to this deadly disease. Danny lived high up in the hills, far from the madding crowds, and kept much of his life a secret. He ate only organic food. He worked daily in his beautiful and prolific garden. He cared about his health and kept his body fit. One day he woke up in a health crisis and was forced to divulge his secret HIV status. His rounds of hospitalizations began.

Danny spent a year in and out of the hospital. Gradually his friends and neighbors understood why. In rural America, these things "don't happen." Even now, an AIDS diagnosis still maintains a taboo aura.

As with so many young people whose lives are cut short by illness, Danny was not going to let go easily. Month after month, he watched the slow and painful deterioration of his body. The time to surrender to the disease arrived during hospitalization. Daily, Danny was surrounded by loving friends, many of them singers, and intimate concerts were performed at his bedside.

Late one afternoon, his good friend Sarah came running down to the nurses' station to find me. "I think it's happening," she said. "I think he is about to die."

I walked quickly down the hall and then stopped at the door. The soft tones of mixed voices—high and low, male and female, elegantly filled the room. I took a deep breath and began humming along.

We stood prayerfully around Danny's bed for another ten minutes or so. A doctor peeked his head into the room and then tiptoed out with a wistful smile, closing the door gently behind him. Danny had not spoken or moved in days. Suddenly, in an amazing gesture, he lifted his body, raised both arms high above his head as if to begin his final aria, then took a deep and long last breath and collapsed down on his pillow. His final sound was silence.

A CHAMPAGNE TOAST IN THE ICU

Friends, do not despair. Difficult times have come upon us,
but our joy must fill the air.

—*Rabbi Nachman*, 1780

While working in a small rural hospital, I realized that people there usually knew each other in some way. Invariably, a patient is the sister or cousin or mom of a member of the kitchen staff or the brother or partner of a nurse in another department. This particular morning in the ICU, I was attending to Leo. He lay in bed hooked up to the familiar tangle of IV lines and machine wires and struggled, even though the ventilator was breathing for him. Leo was a neighbor of mine and a local restaurant owner. I felt sadness watching him in bed—suddenly a frail and vulnerable old man—never again to be seen joking and serving the public as they arrived for dinner.

Some people tolerate being on a ventilator without much trauma. They are able to maintain a level of awareness that enables control of bodily functions and the ability to communicate with hands or eyes or in writing. For others, being hooked up to a ventilator is so distressing and uncomfortable that body and spirit fight against this technology. They squirm and fidget and thrash and grimace. They attempt to pull out their breathing tubes or IVs. In such a case, a patient must be sedated so that the discomfort, pain and confusion are no longer issues on the conscious level. Once the distressed person is sedated, the medicines and the ventilator—and the doctors and nurses—can do their jobs.

Leo was sedated to ease his agitation. However, the strong medicines used for sedation make it challenging to *wake patients up*, and this was true of Leo. Weaning a person from a ventilator and IV medications is a complex process. It involves spending some days or hours lowering the flow rates of the vital IV medications. The heart rate and blood pressure must be watched closely. The hope is that the body can reclaim basic functions on its own. The ventilator is turned off for a short amount of time every day—sometimes every hour—until breathing comes naturally.

Leo was weaned, and as a result, he eventually *lightened up* —an ICU term for regaining consciousness. His son, Al, and daughter-in-law, Sally, were at his bedside, trying to explain his condition and then courageously asked the question, "Do you want us to take you off life support?"

Leo nodded his head vigorously, yes, as if to say, "Please turn this machine off; please get me out of this position; please get me out of here."

I believe that those close to dying understand. They may not be ready or prepared or want to discuss it, but they do know when it's time. Some will acknowledge they are about to die and are willing to let go, much to the surprise of their families. They are able to say goodbye with a certainty that loved ones remember later.

For Leo and his family, the question became how and when? Al and Sally still needed time to be with Leo and to acknowledge that, more than likely, their dad would die quickly once extubated. For hours they sat at his bedside and told stories. They recalled funny incidents, adolescent disagreements, family festivities and travels.

We hold memories so dearly. We try to grasp for details in the final moments of a life, knowing that memories are all that is left. We want so desperately to remember the stories, at least the positive ones. History is created. The details we cherish and hold and the wisdom that is sifted from the words become the traditions and gifts that are passed on from generation to generation.

Each time I go through this process with a family, I relive memories and stories that I shared with my parents before they died. Each death on the outside of our lives reminds us of the deaths we hold close. Nurses and doctors are not immune to these feelings. Grief is not a linear process. It accompanies us through time and space and often feels most present at unexpected moments. Most medical and nursing schools teach that emotional responses in professional situations should be hidden and controlled. However, according to Dr. Michael Kearney, a palliative care specialist from Ireland, there is a growing body of opinion that proposes a direct link between who we are as individual thinking, feeling human beings and the quality of our work as professionals. In his book, *Mortally Wounded* (1996), Dr. Kearney also discusses the fact that underneath the professional uniforms, there is always a human being experiencing both wounding and healing while working with our "patients." He says,

"As we reach out to the other who is dying, and we help that other person to move into depth, we are simultaneously reaching out to the one who is mortally wounded and suffering in the depths of our own being. At that moment we are not there as altruistic heroes helping the victim other. We and the other are both there as wounded ones, each searching for healing, and in this reaching out and reaching in we become wounded healers to self as we are wounded healers to other. Until we recognize this inner dynamic for ourselves, we will either mistakenly continue to believe that we as caregivers always have the answers to the other people's problems, or, as patients, continue searching in never ending circles for that someone or something 'out there' who will at last take all our pain away." (p.151)

It was late morning and I realized the time had come to extubate Leo, so I began preparations. I called the respiratory therapist in charge of the ventilator and told him we were almost ready. Suddenly Al said, "Wait, he would want his *tallis* around him when he dies, and it's at his house." A *tallis* is a prayer shawl used in Jewish tradition—worn as a reminder of God's commandments. Leo was not deeply religious, but he certainly identified with his Jewish heritage." Do we have time to run and get it?"

"Of course," I answered, "Go home and get it. We will wait."

There is no urgency in death. Once it is understood that death is inevitable, the level of drama tends to calm down. Thankfully, this hospital housed an incredibly human-friendly ICU.

"Can we bring champagne, too?" they asked. "Leo would want a celebration to mark the end of his life."

"Why not!" I exclaimed as the heavy ICU door closed behind Sally, the designated errand runner.

Less than an hour later, Sally returned with the *tallis* and champagne. The *tallis* was gently draped around Leo's bony shoulders. The beautiful white silk with gold and blue embroidery was a sharp contrast to the faded and stained hospital gown, but it symbolized a tradition, an honoring of a life well lived. In a sterile hospital's intensive care unit filled with bells and whistles, IV poles and cardiac monitors, we were about to witness a sacred moment: the last in-breath and the last out-breath of a human being who had lived a full life. We can choose to witness these moments with grace, ceremony and honor—wherever we are. We must take on the responsibility of reminding one another to stop for a moment during our busy day and honor what is real and sacred. Breathing in, life. Breathing out, death.

The moment came to take out the tube and turn off the machine. We had already closed the door. Mitch—the respiratory therapist—and I untaped the tube that forced air into Leo's lungs and prepared the suction catheter to drain any secretions. In a dance that ICU nurses, doctors, and respiratory therapists become quite adept at, we pulled the tube, cleaned up the mess and turned off the machine. Al, Sally and I were quietly singing the Hebrew prayer, the *Sh'ma*, during the extubation, in hope that the blessings of God were the last words heard by this dear man.

Sh'ma Yisrael, Adonai elohenu, Adonai echad.
(Hear, O Israel, the Lord is our God, the Lord is One.)

As we finished singing, Leo exhaled for the last time. His life was over. This moment of ritual in the ICU was a way to acknowledge sadness, pain, forgiveness, gratitude and love. It was a powerful closure of the relationship between a father and son. Al and Sally felt proud of how they responded to a challenging emergency. It was also an opportunity for me and for the hospital staff to acknowledge this rite of passage in the midst of a busy twelve-hour shift.

With the ICU doors still closed, Leo's son Al popped the cork on the champagne bottle. With plastic hospital cups in hand and tears in our eyes, we raised a toast. *Le Chaim! To Life!*

WHEN MORPHINE IS NOT THE SOLUTION

Do not go gentle into that good night,
Old age should burn and rave at close of day;
Rage, rage against the dying of the light.
                        —*Dylan Thomas*

What does it take to die? What does it take to "open in sweet surrender to that luminous lovelight of the One?" (words adapted from a chant of unknown origin). Why is it so hard to let go of this life? Of love? This one and only "reality" that we experience in these particular bodies?

With her long, thick, reddish-brown hair and fair Irish skin, Linda embodied sweetness and fear the night they wheeled her from the emergency room into the ICU. The EMTs had picked her up at home, where she was a home health/hospice patient dying of cancer. In her mid-forties, she felt strongly that she was too young to die. So did her new husband, Donald.

Linda was already on a home IV infusion pump and was receiving 650 milligrams of morphine every hour. She was not a large person. Those who understood the level of that dose were in shock. It is not usual, but neither is it uncommon, for massive amounts of narcotic pain medication to be administered at the end of life, simply to make each moment tolerable. Often, such patients are still awake, alert and able to communicate.

Linda was receiving maximum doses of morphine, plus Fentanyl patches plus Ativan for anxiety. The next step was to give her epidural medication to numb her pain from the waist down. Had her pain receptors just shriveled up? Or could she just not let go? How I felt her fear. She trembled, her eyes darted everywhere in the room, her heart beat fast, and it seemed she wanted to scream and cry and just couldn't.

By her second day in the ICU, Linda had calmed. However, Donald, her husband, had not. He didn't have medicine to ease his stress. Slowly, the difficult story of their lives trickled out. Donald and Linda had moved to the area shortly after they were married, partly to get away from Linda's overly controlling family who were not at all happy about the marriage. With Linda's illness taking over her life and her death imminent, the family was *really* not happy that Donald was Linda's power of attorney for healthcare and would be making the legal decisions. They were at odds. The family wanted Linda to come home—to them. They could not accept her choices and decisions. Linda's anxiety, fear, and tension became clearer as we discovered that her family would be arriving any moment.

At one point that second day, I was alone in the room with Linda. She began to open up emotionally by acknowledging some of her fears and asking questions.

"What's next?" she asked me, out of the blue, as I was fidgeting with her IV lines.

"What do you think is next?" I asked.

"I don't know," she said. "I really just don't know."

I sat down on her bed and gently took her hand. "What are you afraid of?"

When I asked this question, she began to tear up and explained that her greatest fear was not being able to breathe. She feared that her breathing would become too difficult and painful. Linda had lung cancer with metastases to liver and bone. She already had too much pain for any human to tolerate. I tried to soothe some of her fear by explaining that usually in the last stages of dying, patients have enough medicine in their bodies to numb the pain and fear. I assured her that she would not be aware of the struggle for life and breath.

Famous last words.

I will never utter those words again. This woman was on the highest doses of every pain medication known to Western medicine, and still she suffered. At the very end of life, most truly do have enough pain medication and are able to loosen their grip on this reality, which is part of the beauty of morphine, Dilaudid, methadone, Fentanyl and Ativan (to name a few of the major medicines used in end-of-life care).

However, discussing her fears did seem to help Linda relax. Talking about what might happen and when helped with her anxiety. That evening before I left work, she asked me if I would stand her up at the sink and wash her long, flowing hair. What a joy! She had not stood for days, but she wanted her beautiful hair to be clean when her family arrived. We washed her hair as best we could at the little sink in her room and then she sat on the side of the bed while I combed the tangles out for her. It is so often the simple and small acts of kindness that make a huge difference in experiences of illness and dying.

Early the next day, I spoke with Donald and her friend Mary Lou about Linda's journey back and forth to the "other world." She would talk and reach out in her sleep and on occasion smile. Linda awakened as we were talking.

"What did you say about the other world?" she wanted to know. She wanted reassurance, details and ideas about that reality, too. Linda knew she was dying, but she could only talk about it in small measures. She would listen carefully and then gaze off at the TV.

She was clearly working at understanding this journey into the un-known.

Close to midnight on Christmas, Linda awoke from what had seemed like a deep coma and said, "Oh, I'm still here." Her family was at her side, tearfully nodding yes. It was her mother's birthday as well as Christmas, and Linda looked at her mother thoughtfully and said, "I guess there isn't supposed to be a birth and a death on the same day."

The following morning I was at the desk in the ICU. As Linda traveled in and out of consciousness, she chanted, "Take me, Lord, take me, Lord, take me." Then suddenly I heard a scream, "Help me, Redwing, help me!" I grabbed a syringe of medicine and went running into Linda's room. I then stopped in my own tracks. I was witnessing the epitome of human suffering in the face of death, and there were no drugs to cure it or heal it.

"Linda, my dear," I said as I calmly touched her heart with one hand and then took her hand in mine, "I am here to help you, to hold you, to let you go. You are not alone. You are loved."

It seemed that Linda's spirit floated in the air for several minutes. She breathed those final long drawn-out breaths, and then a very long pause. A few more short quick breaths…then another pause. Finally, despite her fears, it seemed that Linda chose to stand firmly on this side of the abyss, on the edge of the cliff called Life, and leap valiant-ly across to the other side. My hope and prayer was that she landed gracefully, feet firmly on holy ground, with her halo glistening.

Palliative care is about relieving suffering. We do this with medications and a variety of treatment modalities. Some-times, however, we get caught in the doing and forget that the simple gift of being present—holding a hand, breathing with another, praying, sitting in silence, combing someone's hair—can do more to heal the suffering of the moment than any medicine in our formulary.

LOVE: THE MOST POTENT MEDICINE

Well, I told them, undertakers,
Undertakers, please drive slow.
Cause them bodies you are takin',
How I hate to see them go.
Will the circle be unbroken, by and by, Lord, by and by?
There's a better home awaitin' in the sky, Lord, in the sky.

—*Ada R. Habershon*, from the song "Will the Circle Be Unbroken?"

My father, Alex, was a physician. He spent his life healing and helping people. In the "old school," doctors actually knew their patients and their patients' families quite well. They made house calls and performed every aspect of medicine from treating colds to delivering babies.

My father was also a Russian Jewish holocaust survivor. He escaped from Europe only by the grace of God and the help of close friends and tight workings of the French Resistance movement. This network enabled him to use false papers for travel across the Pyrenees to a ship in Portugal, which ultimately took him to New York.

The stresses of life post-World War II affected everyone differently. For Alex, his workaholism combined with smoking led to his first heart attack at the age of fifty-eight. This wake-up call enabled him to change some of his bad habits, but his heart had weakened and he lived his last years with congestive heart failure.

I believe that often the body's manifestation of disease is related to emotional and spiritual well-being. The fact that my father's heart was his weak organ made sense to me. When the emotional life is a constant challenge and a realm of confusion and uncertainty, the heart is at risk.

~

My mother, Grace, was a nurse. She came from a working-class Irish Catholic family and met my father in the classic doctor-meets-nurse scene at the hospital where my father managed to find an internship once he was settled in America. Grace was a devoted and loving wife and mother who put aside her own dreams in order to raise a family, as did many women of her generation.

My mother's weak system was her mind. Grace battled her shadow side constantly and dealt with depression and anxiety, especially after losing a child she had carried to term. In those years depression was not discussed in polite company. Throughout her life she was haunted by demons and the idea of suicide. In her seventies, she had a series of mini-strokes, and she also lived with constant, undiagnosed abdominal pain.

My parents retired to rural Vermont from a busy suburban life in New Jersey. Alex continued to work in private practice, and Grace was his nurse. The year that Alex turned eighty-two and Grace seventy-nine was a challenging year. He had open-heart surgery and almost died, and she then had a serious stroke.

It was clear to me that I needed to move my parents to California to an assisted-living facility near my home. I spent three weeks in Vermont preparing for a new phase of our lives. I packed for their trip to California. I sent a box of their personal bedding and meaningful belongings to the assisted-living facility, so that their rooms would look familiar and inviting. This turned out to be important and smart. After a grueling airplane trip across the country, with both Alex and Grace incontinent and wearing adult diapers and using walkers, we arrived in their new home, pretending this was "just a vacation." My mother's first words when we opened the door to her room were, "This looks just like my own room." I breathed a huge sigh of relief.

It was also clear to me that one of the reasons I had gone into the field of palliative care–hospice was to assist both of my parents in their dying processes. Months after my parents died, an old friend of theirs told me that she too believed this to be true. I felt strongly that these two beings had come together with love to bring me into this world and that it was part of my path and lesson in life to serve them as they left this world.

Three months after my parents arrived in California, I was at work as the charge nurse on the medical–surgical floor. During my afternoon rounds of patients, I saw a gurney being wheeled down the hall. "Oh, no, another patient to admit." My nurse's mind counted the number of patients on the floor and the number of nurses I had on staff that day. I had not received a call from the ER and did not have a report on this patient. As the gurney approached, I realized it was my mother! I instantly was upset. First, because she was at the hospital and looked so poorly, and second, because I had not been warned by the nursing supervisor. But I had to let go of my reactions just as quickly as the feelings arose.

Grace had suddenly become very sick at the assisted-living facility, spiking a fever of 103 degrees and complaining of severe abdominal pain. She was, in hospital terms, septic. She lay in a hospital bed for four days, drifting in and out of consciousness. Her breathing was labored, and the doctor kindly ordered a morphine drip to keep her comfortable. I sang to her and held her hand. I told her she was going to be with her sisters, who would welcome her, and that I believed she would be in peace. I held the telephone to her ear so that my brother and his daughter could speak to her. She responded with a smile. My sister arrived from southern California and together with our father and my partner, we spent a long, sorrowful day at our mother's bedside. I asked a priest to come and administer the Sacrament of the Sick so that she could die with the blessings of her Catholic roots.

The family left the hospital at eleven at night. Shortly after I arrived home, one of my nurse colleagues called. My mother had passed away peacefully soon after we had left. My first emotions were pain and guilt—why hadn't I stayed with her? But I understood that some people need to let go while alone. My mother led an emotionally troubled life, and I believe that she needed her space to slip away.

After hearing the news, my sister and I got back in the car and drove down the dark country road as the almost-full moon set over the ocean. My instinct was to send prayers to my mother as we drove. We picked up our father and headed back to the hospital. He wanted to enter the room alone. I watched him slowly draw back the curtain that shielded his wife from the open door to the hall. My father was not a religious man. He never went to synagogue and considered himself an atheist. Even so, when he stood at the open curtain, he began to recite the *Sh'ma* and wept. What else could I do but weep along with him and sing the blessing that in Jewish tradition should be the last words we hear: *Sh'ma Yisrael, Adonai elohenu, Adonai echad.*

Religion and spirituality come to the forefront at the end of life. So often those who never considered themselves religious find solace in the familiar teachings of their childhoods and culture. And even for those who were not raised with specific words or prayers, there is often a sense of belonging and connectedness that rises up from the core of the emotional memory. For others, spirit or a sense of the spiritual needs no religious definition or interpretation. During the dying process spirit seems to manifest itself in subtle and powerful ways.

After Grace died, my brother, sister and I hoped my father could now relax and enjoy whatever time he had left. He felt physically well for two weeks, but he became confused mentally. One day my brother and I took him out to lunch, and he said, "OK, what do we do now? Is it time to go home, or go on a trip?" My brother suggested that if he felt up to it by the spring, we might all make a trip to Paris, the city that my father loved the most. At the thought, my father got a sparkle in his eye, and said, "And can we go to a brothel?"

Ah, the mind and memories of an eighty-two-year-old in grief! My brother and I had quite a laugh after we took Alex home for a nap. But travel was not in the bigger plan. Three weeks after my mother died, my father developed shingles. This painful skin rash encircled his upper chest, the area known in Eastern tradition as the heart chakra. Of course, his fragile heart was now truly broken. He had been married for fifty-five years and could not live without his beloved companion.

Alex was hospitalized, and his condition went from bad to worse. His heart failure continued, his kidneys shut down, and within five weeks, he was dying. He became totally confused and did not know where he was. One day he sat on the side of his bed and wept. He expressed to me that nothing he had done in his life was of any significance, aside from raising his children and loving his wife and family. "Love," he said, "is the only thing that is important. It's all that matters." This was a transformational moment in my psyche— significant because for many years, I thought all that mattered to my father was the fact that I had not become a doctor. It brought tears to my eyes to hear the simple truth of this vulnerable man's life.

I knew I needed to take my father home to die. Throughout his

life, he had spent too much time in sterile hospitals. The doctors
(my colleagues) thought this a bit foolhardy as he was so close to
death and it meant constant monitoring at home. Regardless, they
consented and ordered the ambulance.

My father had asked to hear Beethoven's Seventh Symphony before he died. So we played the incredible piece of music over and
over again for the four days that he lingered in the study of my
peaceful country home. He was surrounded by family, friends and
my dog during his last days.

We took turns sleeping on a futon on the floor next to Alex's bed
in order to keep him calm during the night. He experienced recur-
ring episodes in which he would wake suddenly, rattle the bedrails,
try to get out of bed, and repeat, "Come on, let's go. We're going
home. Get the car. The car is in the garage. Come on, let's go. We're
going home."

> People often talk about going home on their deathbeds. It is
> a common phrase and not to be taken literally. All spiritual
> traditions have some notion of home as our final resting
> place. Even without a specific religious or spiritual tradi-
> tion, many innately feel that home means a place of com-
> fort, healing and compassion. Our spirits yearn for this in
> the end.

It was late Monday morning, and I was about to take a break
and go for a quick jog, when I went in to check on him. His breathing had changed and his hands were cool. I knew that he would die
very soon. I called to my nephew and brother. By the time we were
all gathered, my father let out a few quiet, simple breaths, and then
he was gone.

My family stood together as Beethoven's Seventh played in the
background. We let go of parent and roots for the second time in six
weeks. We were orphans in the universe now. I never understood
what that phrase meant until I experienced it in that moment. Our

parents join in union to bring our spirits through to this earthly existence. If we are lucky, they love, protect and care for us until we are able to leave the nest and care for ourselves. And then they, too, have their season and their time to die. In our culture, losing our parents is a significant point of growth and evolution. It is a time to reflect on the depth of creation and the profound meaning of impermanence.

I'M NOT DEAD YET?

Free at last, free at last, thank God Almighty, I'm free at last.
—*African American Spiritual*

The 1960s redirected the lives of many souls. Some dropped out, tuned out or tuned in. "They left what was familiar and headed to lands far from family and old friends to discover what author and anthropologist Angeles Arrien describes as having heart and meaning in our lives" (*The Four-Fold Way*, 1993).

Sue was a child of the '60s. She left Connecticut in search of self in her early twenties, took off her shoes (quite literally), and walked and hitchhiked across the country. She rolled her own tobacco and let the wind carry her. At one point she landed on a commune in southern Oregon where she learned to grow food and farm organically. She was fondly nicknamed "woodchuck," gathering firewood and swinging an ax like nobody's business. She made her way from one commune to another, helping with chores and the tasks of country living.

Needless to say, Sue did not relate to conventional society and certainly did not use Western medicine or visit doctors. So, at forty-two, after feeling a suspicious lump in her breast for several months, she finally made an appointment with a nurse practitioner friend.

She was sent immediately for blood tests, a mammogram and a CT scan. And yes, all of the results were positive. Sue had advanced breast cancer.

> It is said that people die the way they live. I have found this to be true in most cases. If people constantly worry about their health and each and every symptom and pain, they will worry until the end. If people do not accept advice easily, they won't suddenly agree to suggestions regarding their health.

Sue understood the seriousness of the disease, but she was not about to change her lifestyle. She declined offers of chemotherapy and radiation. She discovered a practitioner of "live blood microscopy" who determined the stage of distress in her immune system. She followed his ideas and took various herbs and supplements. She mostly stopped smoking tobacco and drinking beer, and she adhered to a strict vegetarian diet. For about two years, Sue lived what she considered a high-quality life. She then became really sick.

By the time the cancer had metastasized to her bones, Sue was in excruciating pain. She had difficulty moving around—walking, and changing position. She talked openly about her acceptance of death, but she also was open to using Western medicine to relieve her severe pain. For the last few months of her life, Sue became a hospice patient and was taken care of by a home health–hospice team and her friends.

One day Sue's pain became a twenty on the scale of one to ten. She was brought to the hospital for an epidural infusion. Epidural pain management can only be administered in a hospital and must be constantly monitored by medical personnel. Even though Sue wanted to die in her peaceful home looking out the window at her lush garden, she accepted the need to be in a hospital in order for her suffering to be relieved. Once admitted to the hospital, she received an intravenous morphine drip, along with the epidural infusion.

These both needed to be increased regularly.

Toward the end of life, a drawing inward is common. Surroundings and things matter less and less. Attachments to the material plane loosen. Even attachments to people can change. As one goes inside, the outer world gets smaller and less important. The external environment loses meaning as the internal process of dying takes over. So for Sue, being in a hospital ceased to matter.

Sue's room was always full of family from Connecticut and friends who circled her bed and chanted, sang, prayed and meditated. One day in the midst of a meditation, the anesthesiologist walked into the room. I'd love to have a photo of his face when he saw all the people praying and chanting for Sue. He politely said, "Excuse me," and backed out of the room.

Later that night, after everyone had gone home, I sat at Sue's bedside, holding her hand. Her breathing was labored and irregular. Suddenly she took a big, deep breath, and I thought this was the end. I, too, took a long deep breath, when suddenly Sue gulped more air, opened her eyes, looked straight at me and said, "I'm not dead yet?"

Laughing, I said, "No, my dear friend, you're not dead yet."

"I never imagined it would be this hard to die," she said, a few stray tears rolling down her cheeks.

"What is so hard about it?" I asked.

Sue thought for a minute and then said, "There is so much love in the room. Why would I want to leave that?"

I asked if she was still in pain, and she said yes. I received doctor's orders to increase her morphine infusion, hoping that if she were comfortable enough, she might be able to let go. Another twenty-four hours went by and her breathing did slow down, as did her heart rate. Sue was able to say meaningful goodbyes to all of her friends and family. And then, with only two people at her bedside, she took one very last breath and slipped out of her body. She was free from suffering at last.

CHOOSE LIFE

Peace is the bread we break,
Love is the river rolling,
Life is a chance we take
When we make this earth our home.
—*Fred Small*, from the song "Peace Is…"

No one wants to die at twenty-eight years old, and Melissa was no exception. She was just understanding her passions and formulating her life's dreams. She knew that she wanted to be a writer, and was off to a great start as a journalist for a major newspaper. But Melissa was diagnosed with malignant sarcoma, at age twenty-three, and despite the newest and best treatment protocols available, her disease could not be arrested.

Melissa's last weeks of life were spent in a hospital. She had not wanted to die in a hospital—she wanted to be home with her boyfriend and her dog. She had not been referred to hospice as yet, because she needed to believe that there might be one more treatment option, one more clinical trial, one more chance to live a longer life. On April 2, 2010, when her pain became so excruciating that she could not walk or stand or tolerate one more moment of pain that she later described as 100 on a scale of 1-10, she allowed one of her friends to call the ambulance. She knew she needed medical attention, even though she was afraid that a hospital admission might mean another major change in her life.

Indeed it did. Melissa spent two days in unbearable pain on a medical floor, waiting to be assessed by the pain management team. Finally, on the third day, just as her pain was subsiding and she felt more able to cope with the situation, she began having difficulty breathing. This landed her in the ICU, on high-dose oxygen and IV drips and fearful that she was actually dying.

Melissa had worked with practitioners in every discipline: oncologists, palliative care physicians, psychologists, nurses, social workers and art therapists. Everyone loved her and had attachments to the so-called outcome of her disease process. This created challenges in the hospital, where the hospital team members, who did not know her very well, were suddenly the people making the decisions about the final days of her life. Input was received from her various outpatient team members. Her family and friends had their opinions about how to treat Melissa in the last phase of her life as well.

> This can be sticky ground for healthcare practitioners. Everyone tries hard to do the best possible job, and yet the emotional and spiritual elements of the dying process of a twenty-eight-year-old must be weighed equally with the medical needs. This is often difficult to do in a hospital setting, where professionals must be aware of the needs of other patients and families, the hospital policies and protocols, and the goals of treatment. A challenging juggling act can ensue.

> If comfort is the goal of treatment and a patient's pain cannot be managed with routine high-dose medications, decisions about conscious sedation may be considered. This requires tactful conversation between healthcare profes-

sionals, patients, and friends and family. Everyone must understand that providing this level of pain medicine will finally achieve the comfort level required to let go, but it also means that loved ones must let go of interacting, other than through meditation, prayer or touch.

Melissa did end up requiring this level of medication. I visited Melissa on one of the last days that she was conscious and able to have coherent conversations. I was in my usual hurry as I was late for a meeting back at my office. Trying to keep my professional hat on, I told her I was just there to say hello and I did not want to interrupt her time with her friends. She shifted her oxygen mask up on her face and said, "But I need to talk to you."

She sent her friends away from the bedside and motioned me to come close to her. I put one hand over her heart and with the other gently stroked her hair. She held my hand tightly and with her huge green eyes, looked directly into my eyes. "I felt so proud of myself the other day," she began. "I felt ready to go, and I sensed that when I went to sleep that night, I would die. I was afraid, and I asked my brother to stay, which he did. But then in the morning, I woke up. Now I'm still here, and it's so confusing. I don't know why God wants me to stay."

"You are so brave, Melissa, and such a teacher to everyone. Perhaps you still have more to teach."

"How?" she implored.

"Most of your friends have never witnessed anyone dying before. You are so eloquent in how you describe your pain and suffering. Your heart and spirit are so open to everyone who enters this room. You are still gracious to the nurses and doctors and express your gratitude to them for assisting you. You are teaching us all about suffering and hope and love and compassion. You didn't need to read the book *The Four Things That Matter Most* (Ira Byock, 2004). You are doing all the things the book describes on your own—asking for and offering forgiveness, expressing appreciation and love, and saying goodbye. Your life and death are important lessons for so many."

Melissa looked at me with a faint smile. "I didn't understand what people meant by telling me I was brave until last week, on Easter Sunday, when my pain was so unbearable. The technicians were trying to move me to a gurney, and all I wanted to do was scream to the heavens. And then I turned to my best friend, Betty, and saw her looking at me in such fear. I told her that even though this was the most horrific experience of my life, I was still happy I was alive. No matter how much pain or suffering, I would choose life. If that's what it means to be brave, then I guess I do understand."

"Yes, Melissa, my dear, your willingness to engage fully in every moment of life in the face of this intense level of suffering is brave. Many people study contemplative practices for years, trying to achieve peace with the fact that we are mortal souls who live, suffer and die. You embody this naturally, and I thank you for your teachings."

"And I thank you for your presence in my life," Melissa whispered, as we slowly let go of each other's hands.

I walked into the hallway outside of her hospital suite, where her friends were gathered. We talked for a few minutes about how precious this time was for everyone. I continued down the hall with tears falling, knowing I had said my final goodbye—not as her nurse or a member of her professional team, but as another human who had been touched deeply by the power of this young person who had attained such wisdom in such a short life on earth.

When our professional lives are overly stressful, we can tend to take out our own grief, frustration or anger on each other. There will always be disagreements about the best way to care for patients. Yet when a patient is dying, it is imperative that we, too, take time for deep breaths, for looking at the bigger picture of what is truly important, for offering our hearts and hands as well as our expertise. Sometimes it even means taking off our professional hats for a moment and simply "being" at the bedside. A few moments of listening to our inner voices and higher minds can often save us hours of distress. We, too, are "spiritual beings having this human experience" (Teilhard de Chardin).

The Guest House

This being human is a guest house.
Every morning a new arrival.

A joy, a depression, a meanness,
Some momentary awareness comes
As an unexpected visitor.

Welcome and entertain them all!
Even if they're a crowd of sorrows,
Who violently sweep your house
Empty of its furniture,
Still, treat each guest honorably.
He may be clearing you out
For some new delight.

The dark thought, the shame, the malice,
Meet them at the door laughing and invite them in.

Be grateful for whoever comes,
Because each has been sent
As a guide from beyond.

—Rumi

Part Two

INGREDIENTS FOR EASING SUFFERING:
WISDOM, HUMOR, LOVE

STORIES OF PEOPLE WHO DIED IN RESIDENTIAL FACILITIES

I'm not afraid of death.
I just don't want to be there when it happens.
—*Woody Allen*

"Just don't ever put me in a nursing home." This plea was heard by many baby boomers from their parents and grand-parents, aunts and uncles. For those who have experienced walking into a traditional U.S. skilled nursing facility (a.k.a. nursing home), the feelings that arise are probably similar—a mixture of sadness, fear and repulsion, coupled with the desire to scream, "Please don't let me end up here." In 2007, statistics showed that 1.5 million Americans lived in nursing homes and twenty-five percent of yearly deaths occurred in some type of residential facility. Hospital case managers, social workers and RN discharge planners often have no choice other than to place a patient in such a facility. A wide range of emotions can arise for the patient and their families during admission to a residence that will likely be "home" until the end of life.

There are significant differences between *skilled nursing, residential care, assisted living* and *residential hospice*. Within these broader terms, there are more specific categories, such as *continuous care communities, independent living communities, residential care for the chronically ill* or *for the elderly,* and basic *retirement communities.* It is critical that individuals understand all of their choices and the associated costs. There are online resource guides and many nonprofit organizations to help with these choices.

🖎

The stories in this section took place in residential facilities that are attempting to come up to speed with the cultural changes and demands of those who want their golden years to be truly golden, even if they cannot remain at home. Baby boomers are beginning to ask important questions about quality of life, even if the quantity is limited. They will demand creative alternatives to hospitals and nursing homes as well as creative thinking from their doctors, nurses, case managers and social workers.

New models of holistic and affordable care must be created and replicated quickly in order to serve the millions of aging people in this country. A few models already exist, such as the Eden Alternative in New York State and the Green House projects around the country. In addition, many individual residential hospices and care facilities have made it their mission to create environments of care and compassion. It will take the voices and demands of healthcare providers and consumers to create a major culture change in long-term care facilities.

Most of us probably feel as though we would never willingly leave our homes at the end of our lives. However, many of us will not have a choice. We must all work to create environments where peaceful deaths can occur and suffering can be relieved and at prices that are affordable.

Education is the key. All levels of care providers in residential facilities must be educated about issues of palliative and end-of-life care—from the executive directors to the intake staff to the nurses, doctors, and of course, the front-line attendant caregivers. Regardless of position, it should be a job requirement to complete a course in end-of-life care.

The California Culture Change Coalition web site puts it well:

> There is a growing movement across the United States to fundamentally change the way nursing homes operate. *Culture change* is the term that is used to describe the transformational change that many nursing homes are beginning to embrace. While some advocates for the elderly would just as soon eliminate nursing homes entirely in favor of home and community-based care, the 'culture change' movement recognizes the need for nursing homes in the continuum of care, but seeks to dramatically alter the way in which that care is delivered. (www.calculturechange.org; see Resources)

Residents in facilities and their families and friends must be educated as well. They need to know their rights. If the aesthetics of the environment are important, they must make it known. It is hard to leave the sanctity of home. When forgetfulness and lost capacity to perform activities of daily living take hold, there is safety in the familiar. How can a room or a common living area in a facility feel like a home? How can a plan of care be crafted to meet emotional, spiritual and psychosocial needs adequately?

The following stories allow a glimpse into the lives of those who have lived and died in residential care facilities that were nurturing, positive environments. Part of our jobs as healthcare professionals and patient advocates is to assist people in making difficult choices about where to spend the last days, months or years of their lives.

≁

IDEAS TO CONSIDER

In order to become educated in the available choices for residential care, please consider the following:

- Visit the residential facilities in your city or town.
- Read their mission statements and philosophies of care.
- Spend time at each facility and assess the reality of how its mission is carried out. Meet the director and staff.
- Some places have great brochures and look fantastic on paper, but are the workers happy? Talk to them. Are they paid decently? Are they trained? Do they have benefits? Is the facility truly able to provide the level of service advertised?
- Are there nurses on staff? Do doctors actually come to the facility?
- Are the residents happy, clean, and respected?
- Has the facility worked with the Culture Change Coalition?
- Do they use the POLST (Physician Orders for Life-Sustaining Treatment) form?
- Do they have a hospice waiver?

ROOT BEER AND MORPHINE

A cheerful heart is good medicine.
—*King Solomon* (Proverbs 17:22)

Visiting a typical nursing home in the United States can be depressing. Often, elders in wheelchairs are lined up along drab and unattractive hallways. Some are mumbling to themselves or others and do not look particularly inspired or happy. The usual reaction from a visitor includes such comments as, "This place feels scary, it smells horrible, it doesn't feel like home," or, "I would *never* want to be stuck in a place like this." Dr. Bill Thomas, in his work with the Eden Alternative, maintains that you can judge a culture by the way it takes care of its elders. If we judge the United States by this standard, our culture is in dire straits.

Luckily, there are exceptions to all rules and stereotypes.

Grove Park (GP) is a residential care facility that opened in 2003. The owners' mission is to make a difference in the lives of elders, in part by creating a holistic hospice and palliative care unit. I spent a year assisting them in manifesting this vision.

The first official hospice resident at GP was a sixty-year-old woman named Sarah. I met her in the hospital after she had been given a prognosis of one week to live, by a doctor who was not particularly tactful. Sarah felt angry and betrayed. She was too sick to return home—her son was her caretaker and he worked a full-time job. She expressed her desire to live in a safe environment that provided adequate medical and nursing care and was also beautiful and comforting during her dying days.

Sarah was exhausted from years of cancer treatment. She had a naso-gastric tube that was hooked to a small and constantly running suction machine. This was necessary because of a large intestinal blockage that caused pain and irritation if anything passed through her digestive tract. Therefore, even sips of liquid would be sucked back out by the machine.

The first week she was with us, she seemed relaxed and less anxious and angry. She appreciated her amazing friends who visited with her daily and her son who was a devoted and loving caregiver. Sarah had been "spiritual" throughout her life. She practiced meditation and was open to and aware of many spiritual traditions. One day she proudly remarked that she received visits from teachers of Buddhist, Jewish, Catholic, and Pagan traditions.

I was going to be out of town during her first weekend at Grove Park and was a bit nervous that she would not be there when I returned. I said my goodbye for the weekend, knowing that anything could happen. As I was leaving her room, Sarah asked me when Rosh Hashanah, the Jewish New Year, would be. I said it was late that year, almost a month away. It was clear that she was asking because she wanted to live until then. I hugged her and left the room, thinking she could not possibly live another month. The doctors did not even think she would last a week.

When I arrived back at work on Monday morning, I immediately walked down the hall to Sarah's room. There she was, sitting up in bed, looking out the window. She smiled when I arrived and beckoned me to sit down on her bed and chat. "Redwing," she said, "I found an illicit pleasure."

"Do tell," I said smiling, anxious to hear what illicit pleasure was discovered by a woman who could not get out of bed and was dying.

"Stewart's Root Beer," Sarah said. "It tastes SO delicious in my mouth, and once I swallow it, it just comes back out the tube. It doesn't hurt my stomach, and it makes me so happy to drink it."

Contrary to what the doctors had told Sarah, she lived six weeks. One afternoon I asked Sarah if I could take her picture. She loved the idea and grabbed her teddy bear and Stewart's Root Beer and said, "We should make a commercial. I was supposed to die weeks ago, but thanks to Stewart's Root Beer, I'm still alive!!"

Simple pleasures spring up along the road of life, even at the end of the road. It is a blessing to embrace the positive in the most difficult times. It is an even greater blessing to find the ability to maintain a sense of lightness and humor.

Sarah experienced great days and difficult days at GP. As is typical for so many at the end of life, Sarah's world got smaller and smaller each week. When she arrived, she imagined wheeling down the hall to the bathroom regularly and out to the patio to take in the air and sunshine. After only a few days, she stopped leaving her room. Eventually she discouraged visitors and even began turning friends away. At the end, she wanted only her son and closest friends at her bedside.

> It helps to have professionals act as the gatekeepers. They have the authority to announce that visitors are not welcome that day. It is hard for the sick or dying patient to turn friends away, but it is necessary in order to conserve energy for the people and tasks that are most meaningful.

One morning an old friend of Sarah's showed up for a visit. I walked down to her room to see if she was awake and to announce the friend. When Sarah heard the visitor's name, a puzzled look spread across her face. "We weren't close friends while I was living.

Why would I want to see him when I am dying?"

As Rosh Hashanah grew near, Sarah's days became very difficult. She suffered from terminal agitation, a syndrome that evokes
extreme anxiousness, expressed by the inability to find comfort
physically and often includes yelling, disconcerting hallucinations,
and shortness of breath. In her agitated state, Sarah would play out
a murder scene in her head and talk about guns and killing people,
none of which had been a reality of her life, even remotely. We do
not know what causes these hallucinations and agitation, but sometimes even the strongest medications fail to control the symptoms.
It is particularly upsetting to the afflicted patient's loved ones, as a
complete personality change occurs. In addition it is almost impossible to communicate with someone in such a state.

After a few days and many medication changes, Sarah entered
a comatose state that lasted for about eight hours. She no longer
opened her eyes or responded to people in the room. Her breathing
and heart rate slowed. One of the nursing assistants realized she was
about to take her last breath and called to me at the nurses' station.
I hurried down the hall and we stood together, breathing calmly, as
Sarah peacefully died. It was the day after Rosh Hashanah.

The necessary phone calls were made, and two of Sarah's close
friends came to participate in a ritual bathing of Sarah's body—a
lovely form of closure to the physical and spiritual essence. Many
traditions have specific rituals to cleanse the body of the deceased.
Since Sarah had an eclectic spiritual background, when I spoke with
her about this before she died, she agreed that we should be creative.
We put her favorite essential oils in bowls filled with warm water.
There were five women surrounding her body, and we each took a
clean cloth, dipped it in the waters and washed a part of her still-
warm body. Candles burned and music played softly in the background. We acknowledged how powerfully we still felt her presence
in the room.

When we were done, and the representatives from the mortuary arrived, we performed another wonderful and simple ceremony that I had learned at Zen Hospice Project. All of Sarah's caregivers and friends, as well as other residents, formed two long lines from her room to the doorway of the facility. We had bowls of dried rose petals from which everyone took a handful. As Sarah's body was wheeled away, we each tossed petals onto her. This gesture of beauty sweetens the air and allows one last moment of connection to the Spirit who has passed on.

THE MOST UNLIKELY COUPLE

Matchmaker, matchmaker, make me a match.
Find me a find, catch me a catch.

—*Bock & Harnick*, from *Fiddler on the Roof*

A t the end of our lives, we may be required to let go of everything, especially of control. First, we lose our health. This process is different for everyone. For some it is a slow and gradual loss and for others a sudden insult. We lose the ability to perform basic physical acts. Eventually we no longer can perform activities of daily living, such as bathing, grooming, shopping, preparing meals, feeding ourselves or maintaining basic hygiene. Sometimes, we lose our minds, our feelings, our thoughts and our ideas. Other times we lose our friends and our loved ones, simply because they cannot deal with us. Often this letting go and loss does not happen in a clear or linear fashion. We can do something on Monday but not on Tuesday. We are in pain for weeks, and then we are not in pain for weeks. None of this makes sense, and we yearn to have logic and reason rule our world.

It is a challenge to leave the sanctity and familiarity of the home and move to a live-in facility at a time in life when comfort is a priority. In Buddhism there is a teaching called the Nine Contemplations of Atisha that warns us that nothing, absolutely nothing, will help us at the time of death—not our friends or our possessions or our own bodies and minds. We must let go of everything.

And yet for so many, friends and families are not equipped to care for their dying loved ones properly at home. Currently sixty percent of Americans die in hospitals or nursing homes. An important goal for the twenty-first century is to establish affordable residences where people can die with dignity, in peace and at ease.

꿈

Connie was seventy-three when she was diagnosed with end-stage lung cancer that had metastasized to her liver. She lived alone, and her only daughter, Emily, lived an hour from San Francisco. Emily was not able to rearrange her life to be a full-time caregiver. Given the situation, Connie moved into the Guest House, a beautiful old San Francisco Victorian home that had been transformed into a hospice care facility.

> This is a huge issue in our society. The dying require a trained team to provide full-time care. Most family members are not prepared emotionally, physically or financially to take on this task. The cost of 24/7 homecare in most urban areas runs between $10,000 and $20,000 per month and is not covered by insurance. This amount usually makes it prohibitive to keep the critically ill at home.

Connie, a rather proper woman, was accustomed to being in charge and having everything just as she liked it. She did love her beautiful Victorian room and wood-framed state-of-the-art hospital bed, lovely oak dressers and mirrors. On one occasion she was looking at a magazine with a volunteer and started laughing at lingerie advertisements. She whipped off her huge, black lace bra and had the volunteer mount it on the wall with her adult diaper painted pink—an art piece.

Sometimes we are surprised at what we discover about people in the dying process. This prim and proper woman had a wild and slightly naughty side that gradually emerged as she approached the end of her life. A handsome gentleman visited Connie one afternoon and asked if he could take a seat. "Only if I can sit on your lap," she told him, with a devilish sparkle in her eye.

Wesley, the young, gay man in the room next to Connie's, was living with end-stage liver cancer. He was flamboyant and wild in his own ways. He dyed his hair yellow one week, pink the next, and always painted his fingernails. On good days, his friends would dress him up and take him outside in his wheelchair to cruise around the neighborhood. Wesley and Connie became quick friends. When they did not have visitors, they could be found together chatting away, laughing, or sitting quietly watching TV or listening to some of Wesley's wild music.

A more unlikely couple did not exist, but Wesley and Connie grew to love each other deeply with unconditional love that we often witness only when there is nothing to lose but life itself.

One night, Connie became very feverish and lethargic and slipped into a coma. She had not eaten or taken much fluid in days, and it seemed she was close to death. Her daughter was called and asked to drive down to San Francisco. Emily arrived to find her mother unresponsive. She sat at her bedside much of the night, waiting for that final breath. Instead, when the first light appeared in the window, Connie began to moan and opened her eyes. "Where am I?" she asked, confused. The night attendant came in and explained where she was and that she had been sleeping for over a day.

"Bring me something to eat, something good," Connie ordered. Her daughter sat by, astonished that her mother was back in the land of the living. She didn't quite know whether she should feel relieved or worried.

> What happens when someone seems to disappear and become unresponsive and then suddenly return? The truth is, we do not know the answer. This is the mystery of the out-of-body experience. Some go in and out of consciousness and flirt with the Grim Reaper before making that final date.

Once Connie ate a scone and drank some tea, she began to tell us of her dream adventures.

"I was in line at the gate of heaven and was about to see God. My sister was there—the one who has been dead for years. She came to me and said, 'Connie, it's not your turn yet. You still have work to do and lessons to learn. Get back down to earth!' I was confused, because I wanted to go through the pearly gates, but she was very forceful about telling me it was not my time yet. Next thing I knew, here I was, looking around at this pink wallpaper and feeling really hungry."

> Experiences such as this may not seem believable to everyone, but they are to me. Connie is not the only person who has related this type of story to me. The dance of life and death can be filled with surprise, mystical experiences and lessons for all of us, if we allow ourselves to flow with it.

A few weeks later, the Guest House was closed, and Wesley and Connie had to be relocated to another residential care facility. On moving day, neither Connie nor Wesley wanted to get into a car to travel the five blocks to their new residence. Instead, a parade of wheelchairs was formed that included friends, volunteers, two dogs, a life-size boy doll, balloons, candles and songs. We marched down the city street, laughing and carrying on, while passersby wondered what the heck it was about.

Wesley and Connie chose to be roommates until the end. They did not want to be separated and knew that they could support each other during this critical time. Connie only lasted another week, and Wesley was at her side 24/7. Here was a man facing his own mortality imminently, yet he agreed to be the guardian at the gate for this woman whom he had only known for a few months and probably never would have crossed paths with in normal life.

Shift happens.

After Connie's death, Wesley ended up moving two more times—first to a residential hospice in San Francisco and then to Montana, to be with his sister Cathy, his only living relative.

We assume or think we know what our patients, friends, or loved ones would want at the end of life. Most of Wesley's friends assumed that a gay man in San Francisco, who had won awards for his contributions to the gay community and had friends on every street corner, would want to die in San Francisco. But at that point in his life, Wesley wanted the love and comfort of his sister, whom he trusted unconditionally. He no longer needed the wild ways of city streets or the parties at his bedside. He needed a sense of home. About a month after the move, Cathy called to let us know that Wesley had died peacefully, in her home, under a quilt that their grandmother had made.

THE DYING POET

Now I see: living is a kind of slow burning,
And love is what we salvage from the fire.

—*Patrick Clary*, from the poem "Five Tasks of Hospice Nurses"

L ydia was a forty-five-year-old poet. She was an accomplished
writer and performer with a huge following of friends and
lovers, and she was not ready to die.

For many, denial is the only coping mechanism that works
when faced with grave illness or death. Lydia was dying of advanced
metastatic cancer. When she arrived at Grove Park, (GP), it seemed
she had about two or three weeks to live. She did not want help
from anyone. She kept the door of her room closed and only allowed visits from her closest friends. Although she agreed to meet
with a medical hospice team, when the hospice nurse asked her if
she would sign a DNR (do not resuscitate) form, she refused. The
hospice nurse, who had minimal experience, then took me out into
the hall and told me that in his view, Lydia was not an appropriate
patient for hospice care.

"Just because she doesn't want to die?" I asked him. "She is forty-
five years old and in the prime of her life. She has a book waiting to
be published, poetry readings scheduled, friends to love. Of course

she doesn't want to die."

We knew that Lydia was going to die soon, but we did not impose that knowledge onto her because it would only cause more suffering. She was not ready to come to terms with death.

> Our job as hospice and palliative care nurses is to accept and support patients, regardless of where they are in the process. People do not have to be psychologically ready for death to be admitted to hospice services. Some are never ready. I have witnessed others speak endlessly about their imminent deaths, swear up and down that they were ready to go, and then take weeks before actually dying.

> One woman asked what medications she might take to hasten her death, as her pain was almost impossible to completely control. When she was given some options by the hospice team, including going into the hospital for palliative sedation, she chose to stay at home, despite the fact that it prolonged her suffering. Again, it is the responsibility of healthcare professionals to accept the choices that individuals make about life and death.

Lydia resisted death up until her last day on earth. She insisted that she could be in charge of her own medications and let us know what she needed and when. The attendant staff at GP learned to respect this way of being with dying. Many lessons were learned through Lydia. A closed door doesn't necessarily mean a closed heart; it can mean an aching heart. Her pain and suffering surrounding letting go of life were immense, and the only salve was the healing presence of her closest friends.

Lydia lay in a comatose state for about an hour before she died. The friends at her bedside had never witnessed death before and were in need of support. When her death came, they came out of Lydia's room in tears but breathing deep sighs of relief. They asked if we could leave Lydia in the room until the next morning so that others could come and say their goodbyes to the body of the creative spirit that drew them all together. They decorated her room with flowers and candles. Each took a turn coming to the nurse's station for hugs and to tell us yet another wonderful story about the introspective and brilliant woman we had cared for but had not had the privilege of getting to know.

PRECIOUS, PRECIOUS

Blessed be the precious darkness
who shares the night
with her sisters the moon and the starlight.
Precious, precious, precious, precious darkness.

—Song, *author unknown*

Franny was a white-haired, blue-eyed gem. She was seventy-eight and well-preserved, as they say, down to her permanent eyeliner. The sparkle in her brilliant blue eyes lit the room, and her sparse words made you listen up each time she attempted to speak. A power-filled adventurer and independent woman living in Wyoming, she had been flattened by a major stroke in mid-spring. Her boyfriend (also in his seventies) cared for her until he too suffered a stroke and left to live with his sons. Franny needed full care. She could not move her left side, her speech was garbled, and she needed a special puréed diet. Her son Mike, who lived in California, could not provide this level of care, so he brought her to a nursing home outside of San Francisco.

Franny was a tough woman. She had traveled all over the world, trekked through rugged mountains, and learned how to scuba dive in her early seventies. She had maintained a home, gardens and animals for years. She loved animals and plants and being outdoors. Franny was *not* the kind of woman who was going to rest easily in a standard American nursing home. She stopped eating. She barely took fluids. She was agitated, and because the staff felt she was combative, they received orders to medicate her. Therefore, she ate even less and became weaker and increasingly bed bound. Franny was then diagnosed, as are so many incapacitated elders, with failure to thrive. She was referred to hospice, and her son was told she would likely die within a few weeks.

At this point, Mike was told about a new hospice facility in San Francisco, one that perhaps would suit her better. It is difficult watching one's mother deteriorate, and any hope one can offer to make the process more humane is welcomed. Mike was thrilled at what he saw when he visited Grove Park. The environment was beautiful and peaceful, and the staff seemed to really care about the elder residents. Franny was moved from the skilled nursing facility within a couple of days.

Franny could not perform any activities without assistance. Her legs were contracted. She could speak a few words, but they were difficult to understand or did not make sense at all. But when they did, watch out! Franny understood what was going on around her. Of course she was agitated—she felt helpless. After a lifetime of independence, she was suddenly being carted around from one strange place to another, unable to fend for herself. She was terrified, angry and sad. But she was *not* combative, as the nursing home had reported.

Within a few days, we stopped most of the medications that made Franny drowsy and unable to speak or eat. As she became clearer, she smiled more and began to accept help. It was traumatic for her to be turned and cleaned and transferred to a wheelchair, but the nurses' aides worked with her slowly and explained every move. She would scream for a moment and then stop.

A week after Franny arrived at GP, I wheeled her out into the patio garden, where she pointed to different plants and enjoyed eating a raspberry yogurt. Mike appeared through the main doors and looked incredulous, seeing his mother up in a chair, out of doors, and eating, for the first time in months. He came outside, sat down beside her, and took her hand. He had tears in his eyes. She looked at him with what came to be known as her adoring look and said, "My son." He smiled, still amazed at the scene he was experiencing.

"How did this happen?" he asked.

I told him that we had been able to cut way back on her medication and that she was not exhibiting any negative behaviors. It was the philosophy of this institution to try not to overmedicate people. When Franny was in obvious pain, she was given pain medicine. The hospice nurse came regularly to adjust her medicines.

Franny loved company. She loved her stuffed animals. She even loved watching "Animal Planet" on TV. The volunteers and staff loved Franny as well. Gradually her speech became more understandable. Whenever someone whom Franny particularly liked would enter the room, she would open her big blue eyes wide and say, "Precious, precious." This term was used for animals who visited as well as humans.

Franny lived this way for eight more months. At GP, there was a tradition of First Friday Happy Hours. This was a celebration of life for the residents and their friends and families. At one particular celebration, a woman came to play the cello—a treat for everyone. Franny and the other residents sat around the living-dining area, drinking wine and juice and eating lovely gourmet snacks, and listened to the beautiful music. Franny seemed enthralled as she moved her head back and forth in rhythm with the bow of the cello. When the music was over, she sat back in her wheelchair, exclaiming, "Precious, precious, precious."

Franny took the path of long, slow decline in her dying process.

Gradually over time, she ate and drank less and made it clear that she did not wish to be transferred out of bed as much. The pain in her body increased, and she was given more medication to keep her comfortable.

It was March when we all understood that Franny would soon die. One afternoon as I made my rounds, I looked in on her. She appeared to be sleeping peacefully but with very shallow breaths and long apneic pauses. I called Mike and his partner, Steven, and suggested they come in. They arrived an hour or so later and stayed with her until late that night.

The next morning, when Franny took her last breath, one of the caregivers was at her side. Her passing was not dramatic or tense. She simply closed her eyes and let go. Mike and Steven were called, and they came back to GP immediately. We performed a ritual bathing of Franny's body—one last moment of honoring this physical form that carried such a strong and independent spirit for so long.

I will never utter the word *precious* without thinking about Franny and her sparkling blue eyes.

> We all felt satisfied that we had truly provided this elegant woman with some quality time in her last year of life, time that would have been taken from her in the previous nursing home, due to the administration of unnecessary medication. It seemed they were more concerned with keeping her quiet and sedated in order to not cause trouble for the staff.

> Sadly, this happens in facilities more frequently than is admitted. Many skilled nursing facilities are understaffed and cannot provide the time and attention required to understand why an elder might be agitated or yelling. Nursing assistants (the main caregivers in facilities) lack the education or skill to understand the problems of a difficult resident.

Usually RNs or LVNs in these situations are so busy administering pills that they do not have time to sit with a resident and offer alternative methods to calm them. Often the easiest way to control difficult behaviors is through what is called *chemical restraints*.

Our elders deserve better than this. They deserve personalized care, understanding and respect, regardless of their medical or psychological condition. When this is achieved, we will have a more just and humane society.

STRANGE COINCIDENCES

Love each other as ourselves
for We are One.

—*Sufi song*

Imagine a small, pale green room with high ceilings that has just enough floor space for a bed, a night stand and a dresser. There is a tiny closet at one end of the room and large windows that allow beautiful afternoon light to shine through. From the bed, the tops of green and black bamboo can be seen in the patio garden. On the floor of the room, three children color with crayons and laugh. Every now and then, they pick up their picture to show their grandpa who lies in the bed, dying.

Other family members come and go, hanging out in the hall and the common room of this residential care facility. No one was ready for Edward to die, even at eighty-six years old, but he was dying anyway. He had requested to die in peace and not in a hospital. His wife, also eighty-six years old, could not care for him at home, so when they found this residential care facility, they were quite pleased.

Edward's biggest disappointment in the past month had been losing the ability to read. So his family and the volunteers who worked with the hospice residents took turns reading him newspapers, magazine articles, books—whatever was available.

Edward had lived part time in San Francisco and part time in New York—bi-coastal, as the saying goes. Family members had flown to California from a variety of places to witness his passing. Often in connecting with people at a time in life that requires openness, trust and honoring, I seem to also find surprises, coincidences and synchronicities. I knew that Edward had been in academia in New York. From our conversations, I felt quite sure that my brother, also an East Coast academic, must have known him. When I asked my brother on the phone one night if he knew this person, my brother started laughing and asked me why on earth I would ask. I told him I had met Edward and felt that he had a lot in common with my brother.

"Well," my brother laughed, "the year that Liz and I lived in New York City, we sublet his apartment, and your niece's first bed was actually in Edward's top dresser drawer, because we did not have time to buy a crib before she was born."

That was the gold star of coincidences for me. Here I was, taking care of this dying gentle man in a tiny room in a facility in San Francisco, and my niece had been born in his apartment in New York City. YES, we are all connected!

Edward's last days were uneventful in terms of pain management or emotional drama. His family was at his side, and they were all at peace with the process. This sense of peace makes a huge difference. When family members are in denial, afraid, angry, and unwilling to accept the circumstances, it makes the process much more difficult for all involved. The fact that children were playing in Edward's room, behaving as if something quite normal was occurring, was such an immense acknowledgement that death is simply a part of life. The children were not afraid, not hidden behind closed doors, not being hushed because "Grandpa is dying." They were part of the process and a part that sweetened the sadness.

In hospitals, children are often asked to leave or moved out of the room so that nursing and medical personnel can be at the bedside. I remember as a two-year-old, being told that my mother was very, very sick. I was only allowed to wave at her window from the parking lot of the ominous brick hospital building. It made everything about the situation so frightening. It seems important, if we are going to change our ideas about death and dying, to begin with not hiding illness and death from our children.

When I teach workshops about the end of life, I'll ask people to describe their early experiences or memories about death. So often, they say that death was hidden from them. They were not allowed to see the dying person and often were not brought to the funeral. What, then, do we imagine children will understand about this miracle of life, if we continue to hide them from death?

Edward died peacefully in his sleep, during the middle of the night. His devoted wife had finally taken a break to get some rest at home, and his sister from New York had fallen asleep in the chair in his room. She awoke when one of the nursing assistants entered to check on Edward and found that he was not breathing. They did not panic. They stood quietly at his bedside for a few moments and then called the family and the hospice team. When I arrived at work in the morning, children and adults were sitting at his bedside having morning coffee and pastries, awaiting the mortuary attendants.

Months later I received a letter from Edward's sister in New York, telling me that she never knew death could be so serene and how lucky she felt to have witnessed her brother's final moments in such a compassionate setting. She said that the grandchildren saved some of the pictures they had drawn and continue to talk about "Grandpa's special dying room."

LADY LUCK MEETS "THE MAYOR"

They call you lady luck
But there is room for doubt.
At times, you have a very unladylike way
Of running out.
Luck, be a lady tonight.

—*Frank Loesser*, from *Guys and Dolls*

The homeless and drug-addicted community of San Francisco called her "The Mayor." A strong, outspoken woman, Diana had lived much of her adult life on the streets—under freeway overpasses, hidden in the few remaining bushes, and, during good times, in a van with her boyfriend. This woman had suffered her entire life—from an abusive childhood in the south as one of twelve children in a poor African American family to a life of prostitution and drug addiction and homelessness.

Occasionally she had her own residential hotel room in the Mission District. She would spend late nights collecting unwanted food from restaurants and bringing it to the homeless who were sleeping on the cement or cold dirt. She made sure they ate real food, and she collected their dirty needles and exchanged them for clean ones. Diana knew everyone on the streets of San Francisco. Just when it seemed like her life was getting better, she ended up at San Francisco General Hospital with a diagnosis of lung cancer with metastases to her bones.

Then Lady Luck came through for her once again, partly because she was a drug addict with a mental health diagnosis as well as a cancer diagnosis. Some smart city official reasoned that if there were residential facilities that accepted people with mental health issues, it would cost the city a lot less money than continually hospitalizing them. And it happened that GP, the beautiful and high-end residential care facility, had a contract with the city to care for some of these folks. Diana happened to be in the right place at the right time.

For the first time in her life, she was given her own room. She had people to care for her: bring her three meals a day, change her linens, do her laundry and make sure she had the medical care that she needed. Now, many of the other folks in the facility were not exactly like-minded, but she found her friends. The truth was, everyone loved Diana because she emanated love. When I would take her to medical appointments, we would always run into people that she knew from the streets asking her how she was doing. She remembered everyone and knew their stories.

Diana lived on the Hospice and Palliative Care floor of the facility because of her terminal diagnosis. She was determined to live however long and however well she could. She was not ready to accept hospice care and opted instead to go to the hospital for chemotherapy every two weeks. The oncologists who treated her were not ready for her to be under hospice care, either. When a patient wants to try aggressive chemotherapy, most doctors are not going to convince them otherwise.

Serious conflicts arise for many of us in healthcare when the decision to pursue treatment is not based on a patient being well informed. There are very few people who would prefer to let go of life. However, if healthcare professionals took the time and energy to sit with a patient and have an in-depth discussion about fears, feelings about life and death, and the potential harmful effects of a variety of medical treatments, I believe that far fewer people would choose to continue chemotherapy.

On the other hand, many who do continue to suffer through the side effects of these medications are very happy to simply have another day to live. There is no one way to look at this dilemma, but all sides of the story do need to be told. If you sense that a physician is not able to have a serious conversation about all options, ask him or her if there is a palliative care team in their hospital or practice. Often it is the palliative care doctors who have the communication expertise that enables them to have especially difficult conversations with patients and families.

Diana spent each week after chemotherapy as sick as could be—weak, fatigued, vomiting—despite taking medications to prevent this. She received a lot of pain medication just to help cope with her reality; being a drug addict, this was the easy part for her. She never hesitated to ask for pain medication, but now it was because her body needed it to survive.

Months went by, despite the feeling that she could not possibly survive so long. Diana's will to live was amazing. Volunteers would take her out in her wheelchair for burgers (which she could hardly eat as all of her teeth were rotten) or for special juices and vitamins. On the days she could not eat, they would wheel her out in the sunshine so she could say hello to people on the street or stop at a yard sale. She would often come into the living-dining area and make exotic fresh juices with a juicer that a friend had given her. She believed that nurturing herself in this way was an act of self-healing. She always offered everyone a taste of her brews; she never made juice solely for herself.

After six months of chemotherapy, the doctors finally agreed that there were no more medications they could give her. She had already received radiation to shrink a painful tumor on her spine, as well as all of the chemotherapy regimens available. Now it was time for Diana to accept hospice care. The staff at GP facilitated her transition from home care to hospice. By this time, everyone was emotionally attached to Diana. She was someone whom you could not help but love once you opened your heart to her. The fact that she was given the gift of such care and respect in the last year of her life felt karmic—people cannot control the circumstances that lead them into negative patterns and behaviors. Diana was a benevolent and compassionate soul who had been dealt a bad hand. What a blessing that she was able to live her last days at the Ritz, as she called GP.

One night, Diana could not breathe, and her pain became uncontrollable. Even though she was a hospice patient, she demanded to be sent to the hospital. I have come to understand that many people actually feel safer dying in a hospital where nurses are on duty all day and all night. They are able to let go of feeling like a burden.

Diana died at San Francisco General Hospital a few days later, surrounded by two of her caregivers from GP who happened to be visiting.

Her family showed up from all parts of the country for her funeral, including her two sisters who often visited her, her children whom she had not seen in many years, and a host of other relatives. Her memorial was a time of deep grief, spiritual connection, many tears and a recognition of what happens when love bridges the chasm between the different worlds of individuals. There were people of every class and race at Diana's memorial, each knowing her in a different way, and all loving her for her kindness, faith and generosity.

I will never forget her incredibly strong and deep voice, singing Amazing Grace as she wheeled herself down the halls, her deep laugh, her two-inch-long painted fingernails, her love of avocados and her most open and loving heart. I will always think of Diana as the honorary mayor of the streets of San Francisco.

WHAT CANCER?

He who knows, does not speak. He who speaks, does not know.

—*Lao Tzu*

Su-ling was the matriarch of a large Chinese family. Her children and grandchildren were scattered around the world, but when they received notice that she was dying, they all boarded planes and came to San Francisco. Since many Chinese believe that loved ones should not die in the home—as it will bring bad luck to the house— Su-ling's family had moved her to GP once she was admitted to hospice care.

Su-ling's daughter Gina lived near her mother in San Francisco and had cared for her over the past three years since her breast cancer diagnosis. She took her to chemotherapy and radiation and to all of her doctors' appointments. She prepared her daily medications and made sure her mother ate properly and had her personal needs attended to. Gina told me that she never once said the word *cancer* to her mother.

"She would not want to know what is wrong with her," Gina told me. "It is enough that she is willing to be cared for. She is a strong woman with a deep sense of pride."

"Does she know that she is on hospice now and that she does

not have much time left?" I asked so that I would know how to best communicate with Su-ling and her family.

"No," was the response. "She does not need to know that, either."

Once all of the family had arrived from New York and Florida and Los Angeles and Hong Kong, it seemed likely that Su-ling would be able to let go. Even though no one spoke of death or dying, everyone knew that she knew.

One night before I left the facility, I asked the younger members of the family if they had any questions about what might happen over the next couple of days. Indeed they did. None of them had witnessed a death before, and they were able to admit that they were nervous and needed some understanding of the process. The younger generation was not afraid to speak about dying and did not feel that they would necessarily follow in the footsteps of Su-ling in terms of not wanting to know the details of her illness. These young men and women had grown up in Western culture and were aware that some of the older Chinese customs might not fit their new lifestyles.

I gave them an overview of what normally happens to the body as death approaches, and I let them know that Su-ling seemed to be getting very close to the end. They were appreciative of our conversation and later told me how much it had helped them make decisions about whether to stay at their grandmother's bedside or not.

Su-ling passed peacefully, with her son and his daughter on one side of her bed and Gina on the other side holding her hand, calmly and quietly, as she had done throughout her illness. There was no need for words. Everyone acknowledged the loss of this powerful and gracious woman in his or her own subtle way. Once the hospice nurse came and dealt with the necessary details, the large family that had filled the common area of GP for days with their sadness and stories scattered to the winds just as quickly as they had arrived. Again there was no need to linger or hold on—Su-ling was gone.

When we work with patients and families from cultures different from our own, it is important for us to risk asking questions. We do not know all of the customs and beliefs of every culture. Healthcare professionals can make mistakes of protocol, simply because false assumptions are made regarding what people know and don't know about their diagnosis or prognosis. We may direct questions to the patient, when really they want us to speak with the husband or wife or the eldest son or daughter.

The importance of listening cannot be overstated. Spending time getting to know a dying patient's cultural history and beliefs is as important as understanding their medical history. It is the wise and compassionate thing to do—and it may save a lot of suffering for all involved.

TAKE ME HOME

Home is where the heart is.
The hardest part is
Getting there.

—Song, *author unknown*

Lilly—a tall, beautiful thirty-nine-year-old—was dying of metastatic ovarian cancer. She had "fought the good fight" and had tried to protect her family back East by keeping the difficult details of her disease from them. When being admitted to the hospice unit at GP, Lilly called her family to borrow money for residential care. Of course, they were shocked at the news of her condition and flew to California immediately. Her parents were divorced and had not spoken to each other for years, but they both arrived in San Francisco, along with her two brothers. The family was distraught about Lilly's condition and wanted to do whatever they could to help her.

Lilly's parents quarreled over whether or not they should take Lilly back to the hospital for new treatments. They panicked each time she called out in pain and needed more medicine. Lilly had been clear that she did not wish to be hospitalized again. She knew she was dying and had asked, "Please just keep me comfortable." We had brought in a hospice team to manage her pain, and the nursing assistants at GP provided for her physical care.

In her semiconscious state, Lilly started saying, "Take me home; I want to go home." Many say this while dying. It is symbolic language and rarely refers to a physical place. But Lilly's father and brother believed that Lilly meant she needed to travel to her childhood home near Boston, and if that was her last wish, by golly, they were going to fulfill it.

While her mother sat at her bedside wiping Lilly's brow and holding her hand, her father and brother spent their time on cell phones. They tried to contact hospice facilities near Boston, talked to Lilly's doctor about the possibility of her traveling, and called airline and ambulance companies. They were busy. It seemed that keeping busy was their way of coping with the situation and enabled them to focus on something they thought they could control.

When I realized that Lilly was perhaps a day or two away from death, I sat down with the family. She had stopped eating and drinking and could barely move without pain. I communicated to them that I felt the most healing thing they could do now would be to sit with Lilly so that she did not feel alone while she was dying. Her mother agreed. She was upset that Lilly's father insisted on trying to find a way to get Lilly on an airplane.

> People tend to do what makes them feel comfortable when a loved one is dying. In an attempt to control their emotions, some make food, some drink, others make plans, and others take long walks. There are as many ways to grieve as there are humans grieving.

After hours of phone calls to commercial airlines and air ambulances, it finally became clear that taking Lilly to her childhood home was not going to be easy to accomplish. Taking a person on the verge of death on a commercial airplane is a crazy idea. "Would you want her to die on the plane?" I had to ask them. They said that as long as they were with her, it would be okay. Ironically, they had hardly spent any time actually being with her since their arrival in San Francisco.

Her mother sat at her bedside, holding her hand and giving her sips of water and ice. The hospice team and GP staff continued to care for Lilly, offering love and compassion, pain medication, and tender touch. All this occurred while members of her family played out their own dramas for reasons that were difficult for most of us to understand.

Her dad and brother finally came up with a plan they were convinced was going to work. However, the next morning before any calls could be made to ambulances and airlines, Lilly took her last breath.

Once the dying process begins, death will occur. We cannot stop the process once it starts. We cannot change the course of life or death. In our culture, we are so accustomed to "doing things" and yet what is required at the bedside of the dying is simply "being." This establishes a kind of calm that can only be understood once experienced. In our busy world, where there is always something else to do, we must take the advice of Sylvia Boorstein (1996), a vipassana meditation teacher and writer, who recommends to us in the title of one of her books, *Don't Just Do Something, Sit There!*

Say Yes Quickly

Get over it. There's a tear in the fabric
Of forever and it's just the way
It is. God didn't tap you on the back
Because you were a bad girl and today
You pay for it. You did nothing wrong.
It wasn't all the walks you didn't take
Or Irish luck that tossed you headlong
Into cancer. Consider this a wake-
Up call and live your gift of days with joy.
Walk the edge where air is thin and clear,
Where fear can take you further. It's just
Another country. Chin up. Step through the door.
Each breath in a miracle.
Each breath out a letting go.

—*Mary Bradish*, 1997*

*Reprinted with permission

Part Three

REAL LIFE SUPPORT

STORIES OF PEOPLE WHO DIED AT HOME

Life is dying all around me

Death is living all around me

—*Redwing Keyssar*, 1975, from "For Nina in Death Valley"

When the choice is made to die at home with hospice care, it is clear that there is acceptance surrounding the dying process. There is agreement that death is allowed to enter the room. Not to say this acceptance makes the process any easier. Any or all of Elizabeth Kubler-Ross's five stages of grieving—denial, anger, depression, bargaining, acceptance—may happen simultaneously. Regardless, when those dying in their homes state that they do not wish to go back to a hospital, there is a very different sense of spaciousness that evolves.

The stories in Part 3 are about those who have chosen not to die in a hospital, for various reasons. For some, being in familiar surroundings, emotionally safe and physically comfortable, was the reason. Some wish to have access to their possessions, plants, animals, and friends. They wish to create a sense of the sacred in their environment as they prepare for their final journey in this body. For others in this situation, there is a deep understanding that death is not a medical event or an emergency, and being at home allows acknowledgement of this powerful process on their own terms.

Tension and anxiety often accompany death, even in the best of situations. Paula, an acquaintance of mine, attended one of my Being with Dying workshops years ago, with the hope of preparing for the "inevitable someday" in her life. She said during the workshop that her biggest fear around death was that her children would not understand or honor her wishes to die peacefully in her own home and then be cremated in a cardboard coffin that her friends had decorated. She talked about being afraid to discuss her feelings with her adult children because their values were so different from her own. Then, about six months after the workshop, Paula was diagnosed with colon cancer. After one round of chemotherapy, she decided she would rather let go of life than suffer through months of treatment that may or may not cure her disease. To her amazement, her children accepted her decision, and one of her daughters decided to move to California and care for her at home until her death. Paula had two poignant months of living with her daughter. She was able to share her innermost feelings about life and death and let go of her fears and self-created obstacles that had tormented her only a year before.

꞊

Dying at home can be emotionally complex and overwhelming. Friends and family want to help yet find it difficult when there is nothing concrete they can do. Various emotions rise to the surface for both caregivers and care receivers—anger, sadness, guilt, resentment, compassion and love. Our society does not teach people how to do this complicated job. Most do not know what death looks like, aside from television or the movies, and it is a question that people are often afraid to ask. Caring for the dying involves practical tasks that require knowledge and skill, such as turning or bathing a bed-bound person or changing an occupied bed. Transferring a patient to a commode or helping someone sit up to drink so they don't aspirate are not tasks we learn in school. In addition, the job of administering medications can be daunting, and comfort levels with this aspect of care vary greatly.

Tremendous love and energy are necessary to care for a dying loved one at home. In this day and age, financial resources may be required that many do not have. If family members and friends are not able to leave work and be at home, then staff must be hired to attend to the dying. This can be costly. In my current position as the director of a community-based palliative and end-of-life care program, I encounter many terminally ill clients who would like to stay at home but do not understand, or cannot admit, that they are going to need help. It takes time to get to know a client and family. We offer them help in small increments until they can trust and accept the fact that one cannot die at home without appropriate assistance. Unfortunately, often a crisis must occur in order for some to accept the level of care that is required.

Caring for a loved one at home can be difficult and exhausting but also incredibly rewarding. Ask any hospice nurse how they can do their work day after day, and they will tell you it is because of the love, gratitude and invaluable lessons received. When death takes place in an intimate setting with loving friends and family present, the enormous gift of this experience becomes apparent. When there is a conscious choice about how to live and die, witnessing this process can be miraculous and life-altering for all involved.

CHOOSING TO DIE

Cain't no one know at sunrise, how this day is going to end.
Cain't no one know at sunset, if the next day will begin.

—*Y. M. Barnwell*, 1994, from the song "Cain't No One Know"

Alice was a beautiful white-haired, blue-eyed, eighty-eight-year-old woman. She had a deep spiritual life and meditation practice that she had cultivated for the past thirty years. She lived in a beautiful redwood home tucked into the woods. The beds in her garden were built three feet high so that she would never have to bend too low to garden. Oh my, and what a garden! Fruit, vegetables, flowers, trees, rocks, sculptures—a place of solace and beauty in any season.

Alice felt content with her amazing life, yet she was tired of continuing on each day. All of her affairs were in order, and she had asked a few key friends to take care of her earthly possessions. She had also lined up caregivers, if she was to become sick.

But Alice was healthy as a horse. In the fall of 1997, I was to start teaching an eight-week Being with Dying course in my home. Ten friends and neighbors were interested in my work and were eager to examine their own issues around impermanence. Alice called one morning to ask if there was room left to participate in the class. "Of course," I replied.

She then added, "Redwing, you sure as hell better teach me how to die in this class. I'm so ready."

During the evening of Session Six, we were practicing a meditation on dying that many find rather difficult. The meditation consists of visualizing your own death and imagining your body laid out in the wilderness, being disposed of by creatures and the elements. Alice beamed after the meditation. She had always imagined that this was how she might die—she would take a long walk in the forest near her home and just never come back. Her body would be composted into the earth and eaten by the creatures of the wilds.

During the seventh week of the class, one of the participants called to tell me that Alice was in the hospital, having suffered a stroke. Several of us went to see her, and of course, found a feisty woman with few deficits from the stroke. She was demanding that she be discharged from the hospital and allowed to go home. For her, the stroke was simply a sign that her body was ready to let go.

Alice was brought home from the hospital and put to bed. She decided that now it was time to honor her spirit's calling to let go of life. During the first week at home she visited with friends. She ate and drank normally and even walked into her garden a few times. The second week, she stopped eating and did not want any offering of food. During this second week, we held our last session of the Being with Dying class at Alice's house. We brought her into her comfy chair in the living room, and I told her that she was indeed earning an A+ in the class. It did seem that she was learning how to die. She seemed comforted that we were witnessing her dying process.

The following week, Alice stopped taking fluids and getting out of bed. She drifted in and out of consciousness but always seemed peaceful. The minimal pain she complained about was controlled with medicines from the hospice nurses. She had a strong spiritual practice, and all who visited were struck by how incredible it was to witness a human being willing herself to die.

There was nothing left to "do" for Alice. She did not want to be fussed over or fed. She had only asked to be kept clean. Her body was gently massaged and her skin was moisturized with lotions and aromatic oils. Her loved ones meditated at her bedside. They held her hand and sang softly. Alice was also a musician and had taught singing to many local women.

Alice's dying was particularly soulful, due to the fact that she had prepared everyone ahead of time and made sure that all of her personal and practical affairs were in order. There was no need to make calls about final arrangements or guess what she might have wanted. There was no confusion with the medical team about what was best for her. Everything that she wanted and needed had been discussed and put in writing to avoid crisis at the time of her death.

Alice drifted off one morning at sunrise, ten days after she stopped taking fluids. She left with a pale pink sky over a light blue ocean and her friends softly singing.

ANGELS WATCHIN' OVER ME

All night, all day,
Angels watchin' over me, my Lord.
—*Traditional Spiritual*

There seemed barely enough flesh to stretch over Lance's bones. He was a fifty-year-old Vietnam veteran—six feet tall with long, wispy grey hair. His bones seemed as though they might poke through his skin, especially his hips and ribs. I had met Lance several times during his hospital admissions to the ICU for his fragile and failing heart. He was much too young to be so old. Lance was not convinced that Western medicine was the right route for him. He did not want invasive procedures or drastic interventions. He always seemed to be at peace with his failing heart, although the doctors and his family were not. Therefore, he often gave in to their advice. On two occasions, Lance was flown from our small rural hospital to a larger urban one where he could undergo a cardiac catheterization. He also had an AICD—a mechanism that shocks the heart if it develops a lethal arrhythmia. Many Western medical interventions such as these are designed to save lives at all costs.

One afternoon I was sent to visit Lance in his home. He was now a hospice patient and lay in bed looking like he had fought in one too many wars. His skin was grey and he struggled for each breath, coughing vigorously when he inhaled deeply. And yet there was a bright light that shone from his large sunken eyes that made him look strong, open and beautiful. Lance was grateful for every kindness offered to him. "Lance," I told him, "your heart and lungs just aren't working anymore, and this time, we're not sending you away to another hospital. I'm here to make sure that you're not in pain and to see if you need anything."

"Thank you so much, thank you so much, you and all the nurses are so kind to me," Lance whispered in his hoarse voice.

His brother told me later that Lance had lived on $500 a month for many years and yet always considered himself a wealthy man. His mother, through her tears, told me that she had adopted Lance when he was six days old and that the minute she saw him, she knew he was special.

Indeed he was.

Lance had come to the home of his elderly parents to die. His parents were scared and felt they didn't really know what to do or how to help, but they loved their son and it showed. Until the end, Lance hobbled from the bed to the living room and sat upright in a softly upholstered rocking chair surrounded by family and occasional friends and neighbors. They all understood that Lance had made the choice to abstain from further interventions. They all knew deep down that this was the right decision for Lance. He had suffered enough. His family continually expressed appreciation for hospice because they knew he would be able to die peacefully, as hard as this was to accept. Fifty is too young to die, and it never feels right for a parent to lose a child.

During one of my visits, Lance could hardly breathe. He would stop talking mid-sentence and stare for a long while. The accessory muscles in his chest worked hard to maintain a rhythm of life. This was a difficult endeavor, given that Lance's heart had not been able to maintain a regular rhythm without technical assistance.

Ultimately, modern medicine has no machine to prevent death. There is no protocol for immortality. For those who are truly ready to go, one might imagine a bridge, a tunnel, God, a shining light, a river or arms in which to gently fall. When I asked Lance if he was clear about refusing any further intervention, his response was, "Only from God, and the angels."

And so it happened. Despite the medicines, Lance labored for the better part of a day to release his spirit. He turned, twisted, moaned and coughed up blood and foam. His heart pumped as hard as it could. His muscles worked overtime. He was tired of the struggle. He was tired.

I watched this man who was barely breathing smile at anyone who approached his bedside. He told me that God and the angels were waiting for him and he was ready to go. I managed his pain with the prescribed medicines, checked in with his doctor, told the family I would come back and that he did not need to go to the hospital. They were afraid but agreed and told me that if it was too late to come back, I should not worry about them.

It was about eight o'clock that evening when I finished seeing my other patients. I decided to stop by the house on my way home. Lance's mother opened the door, "Oh, I'm so glad you're here," and began to cry. I entered the room where Lance was actively dying. I held his hand and softly sang an old spiritual song, *"Walk in the light, the beautiful light, walk where the dewdrops of mercy shine bright."* Fly with those angels, Lance.

I suggested to his parents that they tell him they love him and say their goodbyes. With tears in their eyes and heaviness in their hearts, they did just that. A few minutes later, I felt Lance fly up out of his body, spread his wings and smile, like an angel.

"Oh, how wonderful that you came back. We just didn't know what to do," his mom muttered through tears. I hugged her and expressed what an honor it was to be there with them as Lance took his last breath.

Death is a surprise visitor, even when we know it's coming. In our society we are not taught how to greet the Grim Reaper or how to act in its presence. Death is surrounded by constant anxiety at the realization that there is nothing more to do. Sitting quietly and doing nothing are not easy tasks in our culture. Often, all that can be done at the death-bed is to allow God (or whatever entity or force you believe in) to intervene and allow the body to let go of life. Hopefully, if we need it, there will be a hand there to hold and help guide our way.

I feel so blessed to have known Lance. He was a man with so little on the material plane but so much love in his heart and soul. He was clear and willing to look at his life and death with equanimity. His faith was strong and his graciousness pure. I couldn't help but think, there at his bedside, that Lance looked a bit like a saint. He had certainly spread love and light everywhere he had gone in his short life. I believe that was his purpose here.

RESOURCES BEYOND THE FLESH

They too, have resources beyond the flesh.
They too, try very hard, not to die.
—*Mary Oliver*, from the poem "Clam"

My only sister, Helene, was ten years older than I. In my mind, she will always be with me as my big sister. Helene was diagnosed with inflammatory breast cancer at age forty-six. She was someone who always took care of medical details in her life—regular check-ups, mammograms, etc. One day she woke up with her right breast unusually red, swollen and sore, so she went to the doctor to have it checked out. "You have mastitis," he told her. "Take these antibiotics." A week later, it had not healed, so they sent her for a mammogram.

"The mammogram looks normal," they told her. "Take more antibiotics."

Two weeks later, the other breast began to swell, and both had the classic *peau d'orange* skin that is associated with certain types of breast cancer. This time she went to a different hospital and saw a different doctor, and sure enough, she was diagnosed with inflammatory breast cancer—the most aggressive type. The new doctor said that her recent mammogram had not been interpreted correctly, as the signs of cancer were evident at the time of the scan. During the month that doctors treated her with antibiotics, her cancer spread from one breast to the other and also to the mediastinum.

How to express the feelings that arise in a situation like this? Anger is too mild a term. Heartbreak is too soft. Fear is the foundation. I think of Wayne Muller's question in his book *How Then, Shall We Live?* (1997): "How can I live, knowing I will die?"

When given an advanced cancer diagnosis, it seems that every alarm and whistle in the mind blares and shouts and signals at the same time. "This can't be true; it can't be me; it's not fair; no, no, no." For my sister, the voice in her head shouted, "I want to live! I have books to write, classes to teach, things to do, places to go, people to see. I can't spend my life undergoing cancer treatment. I have children to raise and grandchildren yet to meet."

Helene had written several books but had several more to write. She had just started her first novel. She was working on major projects in her professional life; she had a son ready to get married and a daughter who was still in high school. She was a communications professor at the University of California, and so yes, she researched everything.

> There are drawbacks, however, to researching cancer on your own—especially online. A study can be found to prove just about any possible treatment outcome. The wealth of accessible information can become confusing and anxiety-producing.

Helene was offered an "experimental" treatment: radical mastectomy followed by radiation, autologous bone marrow harvest, and then extreme high-dose chemotherapy. This would be followed by reinfusion of the bone marrow, otherwise known as a bone marrow transplant. She was told that without this course of treatment, she might live three to six months. With it, perhaps she would live for a few years, but there was not enough statistical evidence to be sure.

Three years versus three months? This was a no-brainer for anyone who enjoys living.

I will spare you the gory details of her double radical mastectomy. Suffice it to say that if I had not been sleeping in her room the night after surgery, she would never have received any relief from her pain. The interns and residents who flooded into her room without the slightest air of compassion knew much less about pain management than I did. They were shocked when I asked for a PCA (patient-controlled analgesia) pump. They acted as if there was not a good reason for Helene to be experiencing "that much pain." I wanted to yell, "You try having your breasts or your balls chopped off, and tell me it doesn't hurt." Instead, I insisted that they call her surgeon and get the proper medications in place.

I strongly suggest an advocate at the bedside—day and night—for anyone having surgery.

Next was the bone marrow transplant—an even more grueling experience. It is a dangerous procedure, and we almost lost her in the midst of it, due to lethal arrhythmias, which can be side effects of the high-dose chemotherapy agents. But Helene had a will of steel. She was *not* going to die.

It's hard to tell the story of Helene's death without the amazing details of the eleven years that she survived, post bone marrow transplant. She was a statistic. No one up until that point had survived inflammatory breast cancer for so many years. But statistical studies do not quantify the power of the human mind and will.

After ten and a half years of struggling, of riding enormous and dangerous waves with occasional moments of easy floating and enjoying life, the metastatic nature of Helene's cancer took over. After being hospitalized for the umpteenth time, her doctor finally admitted, "It's time for hospice." He did not speak to her directly about her feelings or her prognosis. All she understood at that moment was that she was going home and was through with treatment.

She had been in this boat before, or so she thought.

I arrived at her home two days later, with full suitcases, as I did not know how long this next phase would last. Her first question when I walked into her bedroom was, "Am I dying?"

"Yes," I said, "you are dying. And I am here to be with you until the end."

"Why didn't anybody tell me I was dying? Why didn't my doctor tell me?" She cried and cried in my arms.

As I mentioned, my sister had a strong will to live. She was also incredibly stubborn. But several months back, she had summoned her husband, my brother, and me into her living room and, for the first time, broached the subject of the end of life. She sat us down and said, "Look, we didn't grow up with any serious religion and" (looking at me) "I really don't understand what this 'spiritual stuff' is that you talk about. But I do know that without either of these things, it's going to be really hard to die, and I need your help."

This conversation had been the opening. Now, she was close to dying, and whatever that "spiritual stuff" meant, I was committed to being there to help her discover it as best I could.

My sister was a talker throughout her life. It was always hard to get a word in edgewise. As in life, so in death. I joked that her motto now was, "I talk, therefore I am." If she could still talk, even if she didn't make sense, at least she wasn't dead. Friends came to say their last goodbyes. Most of them were clearly awkward as they entered her bedroom. They brought her orchids, her favorite flower, and talked about work as if she were going to be at the office again. One friend picked up a John Grisham novel from her bedside table and said, "Is he dead?" Helene answered, "I'll let you know when I get there."

It was clear to me that she would not let go without saying goodbye to her entire family—our brother and his daughter, and her children. I let them all know that, convenient time or not, they must fly to California.

They all arrived within twenty-four hours. Each spent time alone with Helene, to share feelings and say what matters most: "I forgive you," "please forgive me," "thank you," "I love you, "good-bye." (Originally five things attributed to the lore of hospice nurses, then expanded upon by Dr. Ira Byock in his book, *The Four Things That Matter Most* [2004]). Once she had seen everyone, she began to slip in and out of a comatose state. She continued to talk, however. She held long conversations with people who seemed to be on the other side of the room—her "council of beings." I asked her if she knew any of them by name. She said, "Oh, yes, there's John, and that's Sarah. I don't know them all." They clearly had answers to some of her questions, which appeased her and helped her relax. Sometimes she would speak with them and then turn to me to ask the next question. One day she turned to me and asked, "What part of the Bible are we in now?" Helene had been the Bible reader all through high school, back in the days when religion was still part of public school education.

I hemmed and hawed a bit and said, "Helene, I don't really know the Bible very well."

"Yes you do. What part of the Bible are we in?" she insisted.

I sat quietly for a moment and then I said, "I think we're in the part that says, 'Surely goodness and mercy shall follow you all through your life, and you will be with God forever.'"

"Yes," she said. "That's right. That's where we are."

Helene held on to each difficult breath. She gurgled and struggled for three solid days. I would think, "This can't go on much longer." Then hours later, she would still be lying in bed, barely breathing, and suddenly sit up and demand to go to the bathroom. Several of us would then lift her out of bed onto the commode and then gently lift her back into the bed. Her consciousness waxed and waned.

Finally, near dawn on February 6, from my half-asleep state, I heard her breathing make the final change that I have heard so many times—the longer pauses, something about the quality of the pause, and the long exhalation. I knew there was no going back this time. I woke everyone in the house and told them to come quickly, to be present for her final moments.

We gathered around her bed. I put my mouth close to her ear and whispered, "Helene, we love you, we love you, we love you. Go in love. Go in peace."

Beyond the sliding glass doors of her bedroom, the first glimpse of a new day tinted the night sky, and an owl flew through the trees behind the house. In one of our last conversations, she had described to me in great detail how she had almost died three times.

Yes, it was true. She had had several near-death experiences over the past eleven years. Now, she really had died. I hoped that somehow, in some other realm or level of consciousness, she might still be able to tell me about this time, too.

LUCKY SEVEN

We all go over, to the Other Side
when we've done our time in this land

—*Redwing Keyssar*, from the song "The Other Side,"

As a self-defined death midwife, I have become accustomed to unexpected messages on my answering machine. In late June of 2003, I received a call from a hospice social worker in Marin County. She had been referred to me from someone at the California Coalition for Compassionate Care—I had sat on the steering committee for the state coalition as leader of the Mendocino End of Life Coalition. It turned out that she had a hospice client in Marin County who wanted to come to the glorious and rugged Mendocino coast to die. She asked if she could pass on my contact information to this client and her family. I was still working in the hospital home health department, as well as teaching courses on Spiritual Care of the Dying, so I wondered if I would have time. Of course, I said, "Yes, give them my number."

A few nights later, I listened to another message, this time from Mitch, the brother of the woman who wanted to die in Mendocino. His message was short and to the point, but he did mention that he worked for the Robert Wood Johnson Foundation (RWJ) and that his connections there had led him to me. He was hoping I could help him and his sister. This was an interesting thread of connection for me. I had written a proposal to RWJ just the year before, for funding for one of my nonprofit programs. I called back and left a message and continued this modern game of phone tag.

When I finally spoke with Mitch, he told me a brief version of the extremely complex story of his sister, Louise. She most likely had cancer for some time but had ignored it for many reasons, both psychological and financial. By the time she did see a doctor, her legs were hugely swollen and edematous, her liver was enlarged, she could hardly eat, and the cancer that had been growing in her colon had metastasized to her liver and likely to her bones. She was yellow, weak, and terribly uncomfortable in her body. She had been given two to three months to live.

Louise had fond memories of the spectacular cliffs and headlands of the Mendocino Coast. She told her family—father, mother, brother, and sister—with whom she had very complicated relationships that she wanted to go to Mendocino to die near the ocean. The family really wanted to manifest this last dream for Louise. I understood this desire and went into gear to pave the way for them. I made sure that the official hospice referral was made to our local home health–hospice team so that Louise could be assured proper care and pain management.

Louise's family sincerely respected her wishes and had the means to rent an ocean-front house outside of the town of Mendocino. I met them all at the house for the first time on July 3. When Mitch answered the door, he immediately felt familiar. His language, mannerisms, and expressions made me feel comfortable at once.

Slowly and calmly, I walked into the room where Louise lay in bed—a tall woman whose feet were barely on the mattress. She had dark yellow-orange skin, a sunken face, and a large, pregnant-looking abdomen. I introduced myself and asked if she was up for talking. She motioned for me to sit down next to her bed. We talked for a short while. I wanted to get a sense of her comfort level, what she understood about her disease, and if possible, some clues about her emotional and spiritual state. These are challenging topics for a gravely ill patient, but a lot can be learned in that first meeting. When I told Louise that I would be happy to help her however I could—talking or not, sitting with her or not, doing guided imagery or not—she relaxed.

When I left Louise, she was sleeping and so I began the next round of conversations with her brother and father. It was clear to me, from my experience at the bedsides of many dying patients, that Louise had nowhere near two or three months to live. Her color, breathing and heart rates, pain level, and the fact that she was already drifting in and out of consciousness indicated that in the best-case scenario, she might have two or three weeks. I told this to the family out of respect for their need to process information and also because I knew they all lived far away and were not planning on staying in Mendocino. I gently told them that she was quite close to the end of her life and that they needed to express their love and feelings for her as soon and as completely as possible.

When a loved one is dying, the past is truly the past, and the present moment is all that counts. Despite years of conflict, this family was showing up for an auspicious moment in their lives. They needed to put aside the tangle of family dynamics. They thanked me for my honesty and told me that no other medical person had been as forthright with them about Louise's condition.

Two days later, Louise was an even deeper shade of yellow and too weak to even sit up in bed. She struggled to lean on her elbow or someone else's arm to take a few sips of water or juice. Her pain was well managed with liquid morphine, which her hospice nurse had instructed the family to administer. Louise was in that state that I consider between worlds. She would not respond verbally most of the time, but then she would occasionally wake up and say something that seemed important to her—even if it did not make sense to anyone else.

When I walked into the room, Louise looked at me with jaundiced eyes and motioned with her long, edematous arm and hand, as if dancing, to come close to her side. "Seven," she whispered, nodding her head, "seven." Her father came in and told me that she kept repeating this word and asked me what that meant. I told him I really didn't know but that perhaps it was a lucky number for her. Perhaps she thought that her death would happen in seven days, or at seven o'clock. It did feel like this was a potent message from Louise, even if cryptic.

On Monday morning, shortly after I arrived at work, I received a page from Mitch. I called him immediately, knowing what he was going to say. It was July 7, and Louise had died that morning, just after seven in the morning. She was surrounded by her family, with the white-foamed, blue-green waves of the Mendocino coast crashing to shore in the distance. Her final dream had come true.

WWTD (WHAT WOULD TIKA DO?)

Lovers of truth—rise up!
Let us go toward heaven.
We have seen enough of this world,
It's time to see another.

—Rumi, from the poem "The Birds of Paradise"

PART A: Just one more surgery, March, 2005

On a blustery March afternoon, I found myself driving up the steep hill of upper 21st Street in San Francisco to see yet another possible apartment. I visualized light, quiet, good parking, comfort and safety. I realized as I reached the right-hand curve at the top of the hill that I was on Grand Street, where Bet and Tika lived. At this, I knew I would move there so that I could help care for Tika at the end of her life. Eight months later, shortly before Tika's last surgery, I began my series of visits.

I had known Bet (more than Tika) for many years through another good friend. I had heard about Tika's ovarian cancer diagnosis back in 1999 and of her ongoing treatments and miraculous recoveries. Many women succumb to this particular disease quickly. Not Tika. She had already gone through her first initiation into the world of cancer when she had her breast removed at only twenty-nine. She was a seasoned warrior.

Tika did not fight only for herself. She spent her days, and likely many nights, fighting hard for the legal rights of all people. Her work as the founder and director of Volunteer Legal Services Program (VLSP) for the San Francisco Bar Association was a testament to putting her beliefs, energies and power on the line. A committed and savvy lawyer, she struggled hard for the causes she believed in. She even worked to help victims of hurricane Katrina from her bed, when she was too sick to go to her office. She is credited with making the VLSP of the San Francisco Bay Area the nation's leading pro bono legal services provider for the poor and underserved. Tika fought for social justice for all people, in all ways. She did not give up easily on any front.

I knew quite a lot about Tika: her struggle, her temperament, and her zest for life. I understood she was not going to give up her life easily. For the most part, she did not discuss the severity of her illness or pain. She did not discuss her desires surrounding end-of-life care or what she wanted or did not want. Most people under sixty years old are not planning on dying anytime soon, even those with life-limiting illnesses. Dying is just not in the plan.

> In my experience working with cancer patients, most respond to the initial diagnosis with the gut feeling and fear, "This means I'm going to die." Yes, we are all going to die, but does it take a cancer diagnosis for us to face our mortality here on earth? Can we live each day, each moment, each breath, knowing that the present moment truly is all there is? When Ram Dass first wrote *Be Here Now* (1971), this was a novel idea for Westerners. There is a growing interest in Buddhist teachings and other spiritual traditions that ask us to consider our impermanence on this planet. These teachings open us to the reality that tomorrow's list of things to do will not be relevant if our last breath is taken

today. And who among us will indeed regret that we did not spend more time at the office?

Tika had her fifth major intestinal surgery in November. Her recovery from it was extremely difficult. Weeks went by, and still she could not eat. Her energy waned. Her clothes hung on her thinning body. One sunny San Francisco afternoon between Thanksgiving and Christmas, Tika and I went for a walk, just a block or two, but at least a walk outside.

"I know I'm getting close to the end," she said to me. "I'm so glad you are here. Promise me you will help Bet when the time comes."

"Of course," I said, putting my arm around her small shoulders. "Of course I will help Bet, and help you, in whatever ways I can. This *is* why I moved to the neighborhood, after all."

PART B: One last round of chemo

The "holy daze," as I fondly call them, came and went, and Tika's energy ebbed and flowed. In the middle of the week between Christmas and New Year's Day, Bet and Tika held a small brunch party at their beautiful home. We sat at a perfectly appointed table. Each setting was complete with a new CD created by Bet. We ate a scrumptious meal, told stories, laughed, and carried on. Regardless, the idea of life-limiting illness is like a cloud that always hovers. Of course, everyone is aware of its presence, but as long as it is not raining or snowing, clouds themselves are not threatening. Our work while we are here is to live fully—and Tika was a shining example of that.

One cold and rainy morning in January, Tika got a call that her mother had died the night before. Her mother lived in Los Angeles and was an important part of Tika's life. Until this last surgery in November, in order to protect her, Tika had not told her mother that she had cancer. She traveled with her mother, made visits, and enjoyed life with her. She did not want her own diagnosis to be a burden.

Don't ask, don't tell: It is hard to know whether or not this policy makes sense in any realm of our lives. Is it possible to judge another's reactions and processes when confronted with information that we know will challenge and change them in some way?

Some of Tika's friends felt that, in some strange way, her mother had died so that Tika would be free to let go. They reasoned that her mother knew, on intimate and sacred and inexplicable levels, that her daughter could not bear to go through the process of dying while she (her mother) was still living. There are bonds between mothers and daughters, fathers and sons, lovers, siblings, intimate friends that cannot be measured or understood. Whatever Tika thought about the timing of her mother's death, she did not discuss it.

In addition, Tika began one last round of chemotherapy that January. "Palliative chemotherapy," her doctor called it. The treatment would be given as a comfort measure, in hopes of shrinking one of her tumors. Other physicians and healthcare professionals might consider this a contradiction in terms. The idea that chemotherapy can make someone more comfortable can seem absurd if the body is riddled with disease, the immune system devastated, appetite is gone, and the gut is not functioning. But Tika agreed because she wanted to fight for each breath. She did not wish to give up any hope. If there was a drop of hope or a whisper of a prayer that another kind of chemo could make a positive difference in her life, then by God, who was she to pass up the chance at another day? She was still young, after all.

So she tried it and became extremely sick and tired. She was so weak that she could not go to her mother's funeral in Los Angeles.

PART C: One very last trip to the hospital

Tika lived a few more weeks, riding the waves. On her good days, she could visit with friends and even do a bit of paperwork. On the really good days, she could go for a drive with Bet to the beach or the park. She even went out to dinner with friends or spent time with Marti, her closest friend. Tika lived her life to the fullest every day. She had always been a firm believer in celebrating life, and she took complete advantage of every occasion. Her indomitable spirit was so strong that ten days before she died, she attended a luncheon at which she received a major award. She got up on stage in her suit and signature bow tie and gave a speech of hope and inspiration to hundreds of lawyers and social service providers. Few understood how close this woman was to the end of her journey on earth.

Three days later, Tika underwent her last chemo treatment. At her friend Marti's birthday dinner on February 9, she announced that she was ready to stop Western medical treatment. The next day, I visited, after a call from Marti. Tika was lying in bed and appeared very uncomfortable. Her skin was pale and her dark-rimmed eyes looked sad and tired. She asked, ever so innocently, "What could be causing another blockage?"

"Your cancer," I responded directly.

Tika looked in my eyes with a look that was both deer-in-headlights and the wisdom of someone who knew exactly what was happening but could not possibly speak of it out loud. "We just need to get you as comfortable as we can now," I told her calmly. "I will call the home health nurse, and she will come see you tomorrow. You really do not need to suffer this much, my dear."

Two days later, Marti called again. It was late Friday afternoon, and they were in the emergency room. Tika's pain had escalated, she had been vomiting uncontrollably, and she and Bet were scared. She was not yet a hospice patient. During her recent palliative chemotherapy, her doctor had not prepared her for the fact that she could easily die soon. The frantic call was to ask, "What should we do?"

I spoke slowly and strongly. "What must be decided right now, this minute, is whether or not Tika wants to die at home or in the hospital. If they admit her to the hospital now, she will likely die there. If she is attached to dying at home, then you need to bring her home immediately, and we need to get a hospice team on board. You also need to make sure that the doctor orders the proper medications to keep her comfortable until hospice gets there." Marti said she understood.

> I knew that the home health team I had set them up with would facilitate an easy transition to hospice. However, I have experienced one too many situations when a dying patient is discharged from the hospital without any prescriptions for pain medication. If the hospice team cannot come until the next day, the person is left with considerable suffering for much too long.

The next call was to let me know that Tika stated clearly that she wanted to go home. I agreed to meet them at the house within the hour.

The long weekend vigil began. Tika was made comfortable in her king-size bed, surrounded by the tasteful elegance of the items that make a house a home. She was attended by an amazing group of women who had never participated in a death experience in this way. I spent several hours the first night instructing her attendants about administering medications per the doctor's orders, writing out a caregiver schedule, and explaining the situation to the hospice team. I was Tika's consultant, friend and midwife, and I worked closely with the hospice team to make sure that she was not suffering. Around midnight, once I felt that the night attendants were confident with transferring Tika if she needed to get up and assisting with any needed medications, I went home for a short night's sleep.

Now, mind you, the women attending to Tika were also Amazon warriors. Each one, in her own right, was taking on the struggles of the world. There was not a shy one in the group. However, attending a death is not an everyday life experience. It is like crossing the threshold into a totally unknown territory. Although I could guide them, I could not just hand over a map. Each journey is different, the pitfalls cannot be predicted, and the lessons cannot be outlined ahead of time. Being with dying requires total presence—mind, body, heart and soul.

The vigil continued day and night throughout the weekend. Tika drifted in and out of consciousness, in and out of pain, yet she was able at times to maintain a sense of humor and a sly smile. There were moments of cognition and laughter, poignant moments of love, and moments of heartbreak and tears. Women lounged on her bed, others brought food and drink, and Bet held her close and drifted in and out of sleep with her. Her dearest friend, Jacob, a physician with many years working with the AIDS epidemic and who had lost his own partner, was also at her bedside. Candles burned, prayers were spoken, and toasts were made to an incredible human being who had led a power-filled and loving life. Her medications were increased as needed, to keep her comfortable. The hospice nurses who came to visit were taken aback by the enormous and palpable love and compassion in the house.

Each time I thought she could not hold on much longer, another few hours would go by. I went home to take naps periodically, but being a midwife to the dying means showing up as much as possible. It requires guiding the loved ones through the "deathing" process, just as a birth midwife guides the partner as well as the woman in labor.

Dying is intense labor. Imagine how hard a woman must push to separate her baby from her womb. In dying, we do the opposite—we must push hard to separate the spirit from the body. Just as in birth, many believe that in death the spirit is sent out through a long, dark tunnel or passageway of some kind into a bright and brilliant light. Those remaining at the bedside are awestruck.

Tika died early on Monday morning. The ceremonial feeling of the weekend continued throughout the day, with prayers and song and chanting and the ritual bathing of Tika's body and anointing her with aromatic oils. A wake was held in the evening—a time for friends and family to honor and pay their respects to a life well lived.

These days, people are not accustomed to seeing the body of someone who has died at home, at peace, in their own bed. The funeral industry has created the belief that it is not natural to keep the body at home. The mortuary usually comes and whisks the body away so that we do not have to see what death looks like. This has become mainstream practice since the 1950s. Before that, families took care of their dead and honored them in the place they lived. In my experience, it feels more relaxing for everyone involved, and more natural, to keep the body of the beloved in the sanctity of the home.

When Tika's body was carried out by the gentlemen from the mortuary the next morning, another ceremony took place. There was drumming, singing, tossing of rose petals, and prayers to her spirit as the van that carried her drove down the street.

We cry for the loss of love, the missing of our beloved, and the knowing that some piece of a life will be forgotten over time. Impermanence is not a comforting embrace, but it allows us to sink into the spaciousness of the mystery that both surrounds and fills us.

TWISTS OF FATE

I pray to the Ones
Whose lives are a prayer
That my life too, may be a prayer.

—*Jo McClure*, 1985, from the song "Life is a Prayer,"

I met Joni when I was twenty-five. She had a tough exterior—worked as a park ranger, smoked cigarettes, and drank beer and whiskey. Her working-class background and difficult childhood spurred her into a college degree. Her career path included the use of her sharp brain to speak out against things that were wrong with our society—war, sexism, injustice, cruelty to animals and racism.

Joni was one of many in our rural and politically active community who became involved in Native American struggles for equality and respect. In that process, many also experienced their own spiritual evolution. As in Native American traditions, all life is sacred, and the way we walk on this earth is ultimately what matters most. In her thirties, Joni had joined a group who practiced prayer rituals at every equinox and solstice. She helped create full moon rituals and studied with Native teachers to learn the ritual of the sweat lodge. As she participated in this path, her friends noticed a softening in her being and a different kind of opening in her heart. As the years progressed, Joni started taking better care of herself. She found a new job that she enjoyed. She entered a new relationship. She even contemplated quitting smoking.

Transformations happen in mysterious ways.

The summer before Joni was to turn fifty, I received a phone call with news that she had just been diagnosed with Stage 4 lung cancer. She had been experiencing a worse than usual cough all summer. She finally went to the doctor—reluctantly, due to her inadequate health insurance. The doctor put her on antibiotics. When the cycle of antibiotics was complete and the cough worse, a chest x-ray then showed a huge mass in her right lung. I hung up from the phone call feeling a gamut of emotions: anger at her for smoking and drinking too much, anger at the doctor who gave her antibiotics and did not examine her thoroughly, anger at cancer for taking away so many young people at the prime of life, and anger at myself for not visiting her all the times I had said I would. I knew that her prognosis would not be good, even with chemotherapy.

Joni was a particularly stubborn woman and did not take advice easily. When she was diagnosed, she was living in a small rural town in Oregon, caring for her ninety-year-old aunt, Flora. She was afraid to tell Flora how sick she was and afraid to even go near the feelings that now she would likely die before her aunt did. Who would take care of Flora? So when her friends tried to suggest that she move back to her old community where she would be surrounded by love and support, she said, "Yes, of course, that's a good idea." But she never showed up.

Joni sought out several opinions from various oncologists, none of which were optimistic. She had surgery and a round of chemotherapy that made her feel so sick that she quickly said, "I can't do this treatment. I'd rather get my affairs in order and just be able to die in peace."

It took a month for her to get her affairs in order—paperwork, wills, monies, informing her powers of attorney of the location of her important papers. Then she had to tell Flora of her prognosis. She found someone who could move into her trailer and help her aunt, and finally, she agreed to come to Mendocino for care. Of course, she insisted on driving her truck with a load of her possessions, by herself.

Joni arrived on Monday, October 1, to stay in a small cottage behind a friend's house. Other friends created an impromptu "share the care" team and took turns staying with her. (*Share the Care* is the name of both a wonderful book and a web site that helps people understand how to work together to care for someone who is ill or dying. See Resources and Bibliography.) The local hospice team cared for her medically and managed her pain. She also required medication to deal with the anxiety that arises from shortness of breath and lung cancer. Everyone knew the clear instructions, "DO NOT CALL 911." This is the normal protocol when hospice is on board.

The next Saturday night, one of Joni's closest friends stayed with her. Joni got really short of breath and clutched her chest saying she thought she was having a heart attack. Her friend Sherrie, in a panic, called 911. I received the call to meet them at the hospital. I cursed under my breath the entire thirty-minute drive, wondering why the hell 911 had been called. Everyone, especially Joni, had agreed that if she stopped breathing or her heart stopped, she was NOT to be brought to the hospital. But panic takes over at times. When a loved one thinks they are about to die of a heart attack, the normal tendency is to call for help.

Now, as a nurse at this hospital, I knew all of the emergency room doctors, and I had my preferences. There was a new doctor in town who worked in the ER occasionally, whom I wanted to meet.

I had been told he was a Native American medicine man as well as a Western emergency room doctor. Lo and behold, when I called to see who was on duty that night, it was indeed he, Dr. Frank. Well, I chuckled to myself as I drove madly to meet the ambulance, I guess there was a reason that 911 was called tonight.

The nurse on duty went through all of the mandatory protocols, despite the fact that the 911 call had been a mistake and Joni was a hospice patient and did not want to be in the hospital. Her heart was in a rapid and irregular rhythm, which was why she thought she was having a heart attack. The ER team was debating what to do about it when Dr. Frank walked into the room. I liked him immediately and told him I had looked forward to meeting him. He had heard I was doing spiritual work with the dying and said he had wanted to meet me as well.

I explained what had happened and why Joni was at the ER. I also told him that Joni had spent years doing work with Native Americans at Big Mountain, helping raise money and awareness about tribal struggles, and that her own spirituality was very much influenced by those traditions. I told him that she really did not want to be in the hospital.

He listened attentively and then turned to Joni and asked her if what I had said was true. She nodded yes. He asked her if she understood that if they did not treat her heart symptoms she might die. Was she ready for that? She said yes, she was ready, and she wanted to die at home.

He then did something that I never imagined I would see in an ER. He closed the curtains around her gurney, sat on the stool beside her, and asked if he could sing her a medicine song. Her eyes lit up and she nodded, "Yes, of course, yes." He closed his eyes and chanted for about five minutes. When he opened his eyes, he asked us to please wait while he went and got something. Meanwhile, the ER nurse prepared her discharge paperwork.

When the paperwork was signed and we were ready to leave, Dr. Frank came back into the room with a small leather pouch and took out a bundle of sage—an herb that is burned quite commonly to purify and heal. The pungent smoke surrounds a person or fills a room and is used in many Native American rituals, just as incense is used in other cultures. He handed me the sage and said, "This is special medicine. Please smudge her with it as soon as you get home and every day from now on."

As we wheeled Joni out to the car, I felt like I was in a dream. I had just watched an ER doctor sing to his patient and then give me a prescription for sage to take home. There clearly was a reason why 911 had been called tonight.

Two nights later I arrived at the cottage at sunset to find Joni and another friend sitting outside on the tiny deck, drinking gin and tonics. "To LIFE," they both said. This was her last time out of bed. Her pain suddenly worsened after that night, as did her shortness of breath. The morphine dose was increased by the hospice nurse and Ativan was given for her increasing anxiety.

Her friend Judy was to spend the next night at the cabin with her, but there were a few hours of unscheduled time the following morning. I had managed to find a volunteer from the Cancer Center to cover it and said I would come by and show her what was needed before I went to work. Judy left me a message at seven in the morning, before she left, that Joni's breathing was very labored.

When I arrived at seven-thirty to meet the volunteer, I walked into a room where the only noise was the swishing whisper of the oxygen machine. I looked at Joni from the doorway and could not tell if her chest was rising. As I walked slowly toward her, I clearly saw that it was not and that she had let go of this small shell that was her body. Joni had done it her way, right until the end.

The volunteer left quickly. She had never seen a dead body before and was quite disturbed. I knew she would get support from others at the Cancer Center, so I focused on Joni. I did one last smudge of her body and the room with the sage that Dr. Frank had given me. I then called her close friends to participate in the ritual bathing of her body, dressing her in her favorite clothes, and preparing her to lie in state until that evening, when we would perform a short ceremony around her bed with all who had cared for her.

Carla, the woman who owned the cottage and so generously allowed Joni to stay there, let us know how important it had been to witness the process of Joni's dying and the kind of attention and care that her community of friends brought to such a sad and difficult situation. Little did we know that only a few months later, Carla would go through the experience again, this time with Hal, her husband of fifty-five years.

After Hal died, Carla told her daughter how valuable the lessons of Joni's death had been for her, and how they had enabled her to be present for her husband in a way that she could not have imagined before.

Traditional Navajo Prayer

May it be beautiful before me,
May it be beautiful behind me,
May it be beautiful below me,
May it be beautiful above me,
May it be beautiful all around me.

I am restored in beauty
I am restored in beauty
I am restored in beauty
I am restored in beauty.

RITES OF PASSAGE

I ain't really ready to leave you,
I ain't ready to go.

—*African American Spiritual*

I n most cultures, a spiritual event or rite of passage is marked
with ceremony or ritual: birthdays, weddings, bar mitzvahs,
communion, sweet sixteen, anniversaries, and so forth. Ritual
requires the creation of sacred space. That space is imbued with
meaning, through decorations, lighting, candles, color, art, music,
plants or sometimes silence. Dr. Rachel Remen, in her book *Kitchen
Table Wisdom* (1997), suggests, "Ritual is a way of consecrating the
ordinary." Death is ordinary. It happens every day to many thousands of people, just as birth is ordinary.

A particular death, however, of a person you know, love, and
have cared for personally or professionally, is never an ordinary experience. Witnessing the transformation of a being from life to not-
life, from breathing to not breathing, from heart beating to heart
not beating, is extraordinary. And yet in Western culture, we are not
encouraged and are even hidden from the richness of this profound
moment in life.

As healthcare professionals, we are called in to pronounce the fact that the pulse has stopped and death has occurred. What a different experience it might be to be called in to be present for the last hours or minutes of a person's life and asked to witness their passing before we pronounced the obvious.

⁓

Lara and Sharon were both strong, independent, feisty women and were both clients of my palliative care program. Lara was sixty-one and Sharon was twenty-seven. They both had Stage 4 glioblastomas. Sharon had been dealing with cancer for over a year, Lara for only six months. Each underwent surgery, chemotherapy and radiation. They both had some good months and days during the course of their illnesses, and each desperately wanted to live. During the month before they died, I kept having the feeling they might die on the same day. Luckily for me, their deaths were two days apart.

Lara had already accomplished many of her dreams in life. She was an oral historian, a political activist, a wild woman of the 1960s and '70s who did what she pleased when she pleased.

Lara called the process of her last few months *joy therapy*. Once she understood that this was indeed the end of her life, she decided to make the most of it. She had heard many stories of suffering at the end of life, and her story was to be different. Most days she did not talk about dying. When friends visited, she wanted to speak of life. She created artwork until her last week—colorful collages and detailed drawings. Her vital creative life force flowed through her like a powerful river on a mission to the universal sea.

I visited Lara and her sisters on the morning of her last day. Her extremities were getting cool and her breathing was labored. She barely opened her eyes, and when she did, her consciousness seemed far away and she no longer made contact with those around her. I knew death was imminent but, as always, did not want to make a specific prediction. Lara's nieces were there as well. I went into another room with her sisters, Linda and Leslie, and spoke with them about the dying process as a ritual. They were concerned about too much noise around Lara and too many people. I let them know it was fine to create the kind of ceremonial space that felt right for them. They could light candles, ask for quiet, play Lara's music. One of her nieces brought incense to burn and essential oils to anoint Lara's body and clear the energies in the room when she died. We spoke about a bathing ritual once she passed—a final goodbye to the body that had served Lara so well for sixty-one years.

At Lara's funeral the next weekend, Leslie said to me, "When you shared the idea that death can be a ritual, it made all the difference in the world to me. I had never thought about it that way before. That concept allowed us to have such a beautiful last day together."

Rituals can be as simple as lighting a candle and saying a prayer or sitting in silence or offering a gentle touch. It can be whatever you choose. It is your intention that sanctifies the moment.

Sharon did not have the same peace of knowing she had fulfilled her dreams. At twenty-seven, she was just beginning to formulate dreams and the path she would take to achieve them. Sharon was at the beginning of her adult life and knew it would end quickly. She, too, wanted to live. She wanted a full life with her lover, friends and family. She often spoke of the future, knowing full well how short her future would be. One day at an appointment with her palliative care doctor, she said, "It's not like the idea of dying isn't in the back of my mind all the time. I just don't want to talk about it all the time." She agreed that if she did need a safe space to talk about the hard issues of life and death, this office was the place. She also let me, her palliative care nurse, know that she felt safe talking about some of her troubling thoughts in the safety of her home, where I visited regularly.

Having a palliative care physician and team makes a huge difference in the experience of a life-limiting illness. Not all healthcare professionals are skilled at having difficult conversations, and I am grateful for the ones who are. At the UCSF Symptom Management Service in San Francisco, I have had the privilege of witnessing some of the most difficult patient conversations handled in the most tactful and gracious ways.

Last year, after a physician's presentation at a palliative care conference, I asked him about his experience with oncologists who were not able to have realistic conversations with their patients. He said, "If I need surgery, I want a great surgeon, and they have to work hard to perfect that skill. Not every doctor has what it takes to be a good communicator, and most of them do not have the time or energy to learn those skills. What we need to do is make sure that the doctors who cannot do this part of the work know that there are skilled palliative care clinicians to whom they can refer patients."

Sharon had several months of feeling stable before a sudden and dramatic decline. Her balance became impaired and she had difficulty walking. She had orthostatic hypotension, which worsened over the last weeks, passing out each time she tried to stand up. As she lost control of her facial and tongue muscles, swallowing became increasingly difficult and her speech hard to understand. Her weight dropped to about seventy pounds, but still her spirit was strong.

The night before Sharon died, she sat up for dinner with her family, her boyfriend and her friend Ann. She ate a little bit of food and communicated fairly clearly with everyone. She asked her friend to visit again soon so that she could hear more about Ann's life and work and adventures.

The next morning Sharon did not really wake up. She was still breathing, but she wasn't responding. She drifted into a coma and remained in that state until eleven o'clock that night.

On her queen-sized bed in the small apartment that she shared with her boyfriend Dan, Sharon slowly and peacefully took her final breaths and exited this world. She was surrounded by her loved ones, her cat, her therapist and me. Dan held her for a long time afterwards. I cleared some of the clutter from her bedside so that we could light candles and bathe and dress her in her favorite pajamas and T-shirt. Each ritual at the time of death is different. The energy must be in sync with the dying and those who are left behind. The family decided to keep her body at home overnight and have the mortuary come in the morning. Often, loved ones need this time with the body to fully understand that death has occurred. We stare at this being whom we have loved—wishing, hoping, almost believing that somehow another breath will come.

I spoke to the hospice RN on call and said I would make the official pronouncement. I called the coroner and helped with the official business and then left Sharon's body in the loving arms of her family, to grieve through the night.

This ride called life is unpredictable. We don't know how long our tickets are good for until we reach the final exit. For some, life is a long journey, for others a brief adventure into the experience of earthly embodiment. I have faith that there are reasons for all of the variations of experience, governed by forces much greater than the human brain. We must accept that we have no good answer to the most difficult question—"Why did she or he have to die?"

Mountain Mystery Song

Oh the Great Spirit came and she showed me the way
to the mountains steep and high, and she said,
"If you listen very carefully, I'll tell you a story of the days gone by."
So I stopped and I waited and I listened.
Many suns came up, many moons went down.
I swam in the clear pools, I breathed in the clean air,
I found an owl feather lying on the ground.
"Well the birds that you see flying here, they've flown here since before time began.
And the rocks piled high almost touching the sky, they've been here forever, this is virgin land.
"And all of the mysteries lie inside me," the mountains said clear and strong.
"It's nothing you'll ever know, it's nothing we'll ever show;
just listen to the music of your prayers and your songs."

—*J. Redwing Keyssar,* 1987

BLESSINGS

Hope is the thing with feathers, that perches in the soul
And sings the tune without the words
And never stops at all.

—*Emily Dickinson*

I first visited Betty in July at the request of her brother, Harold. He called our intake department at Jewish Family and Children's Services while he was in San Francisco visiting his sister who had metastatic lung cancer. It seemed obvious to him that she needed help. Betty was a strong, independent, self-employed artist who had lived on her own, traveled the world, and taken good care of herself (except for her smoking habit) all of her adult life. Just because she could hardly walk up the steps to her house or get off the couch did not mean that she now needed care in her home. This attitude is commonly heard during homecare assessments. No one likes to feel dependent.

Betty and her brothers were charming and openhearted people. Her cousins, nieces, nephews and sisters-in-law were an incredible extended family of caregivers, and I instantly fell in love with them all.

When I met Betty she was hoping to continue chemotherapy, which had been temporarily stopped due to an infection. Betty thought that perhaps she could use an attendant caregiver four hours a day once or twice a week. Her brother felt that she needed help every day, but it was agreed that twice a week was a good start. Within two weeks, we were assisting Betty daily due to a slow but progressive decline in her health.

Betty did not want to discuss death or hospice or her prognosis. She even asked her brother not to ask her oncologist about her prognosis. She did not want to let go of her hope for a cure. Hope—yes, that thing with feathers, that precious commodity, without which we cannot live or wake up in the morning or hold onto any of our dreams.

Over the next few months, I visited Betty every few weeks to see how she was doing and to ensure that she was receiving everything she needed from our caregivers.

> As the director of a palliative care program within the context of a social service agency, I have the unique position of being able to offer consistent support to anyone who is a client of our agency at no extra cost. Palliative care is about relieving suffering. One does not have to be a hospice patient in order to receive palliative care. Anyone with a cancer diagnosis, especially an advanced one, is suffering. Betty had a hard time letting go of her independent identity—she was an artist, a photographer, a cook, a gardener and a gatherer of friends. Now she was in need of assistance to accomplish any task, and that was hard for her to accept. Our palliative care team worked with her around these complex emotional and spiritual issues, which were causing her as much pain and suffering as her physical illness.

It wasn't until December, when Betty's oncologist finally admitted that there was nothing more that Western medicine had to offer, that she agreed to have a hospice team see her at home. I worked in conjunction with the team to ensure that Betty received the necessary medication and equipment. Since many hospice nurses do not have the luxury of long appointments and involved conversations, I remained a resource for Betty and her brother regarding the details of the dying process. We had come to know each other over the months and had built a trust and rapport that was a unique and special gift.

Betty was not a religious person although her family was Jewish. As with many Jews in our culture, religion does not always play a strong role. However, other members of her family did have strong religious beliefs, and so the rabbi on our palliative care team worked with Betty and her family to help clarify what parts of tradition they wished to incorporate into the prayers and rituals of her dying process. It was wonderful to see the willingness to discuss these issues ahead of time. Thus, as Betty took each step closer to the end of her life, everyone was prepared, on many levels. They knew which blessings would be said as she was dying and during the ritual bathing of her body. They understood how to orchestrate *shiva*—the week of mourning after a death. And as a family, they heard and accepted each other's feelings about the spiritual journey they were witnessing. Open and honest communication is crucial among the loved ones of the dying.

Betty had so many friends and family members from all across the country wanting to visit her regularly that towards the end, she became a bit overwhelmed. One day she said to her brother, "Let's have a tea party on Saturday and invite everyone to come over at the same time. One last party."

As difficult as it sounded to throw a party, Harold understood Betty's nature and how perfect the idea was. E-mail invitations were sent out and phone calls were made. Goodies were ordered from the finest bakeries, and Harold's wife, Maggie, prepared the perfect tea party. The time was set for three in the afternoon.

At eleven that Saturday morning, Maggie phoned me at home.

"Redwing, her breathing is really different. I'm not totally sure, but I think she is dying. Can you come over?"

"Of course," I said. "I have a few things I must attend to, and then I'll be there."

Less than half an hour later, the phone rang again. Betty had just died. I said I would come right over and assist them with the ritual bathing of her body. Harold and Maggie decided not to cancel the tea party—it would simply serve as a wake.

When I arrived, Betty's body looked more peaceful and at ease than it had in months. No more wrinkles on her brow. No more suffering. The surfaces around her hospital bed were filled with flowers in crystal vases and candles in beautiful holders. We gathered around her bed, and Harold and her cousins read a beautiful Hebrew blessing. Bowls of warm water with her favorite lavender essential oil were brought in from the kitchen, and four women washed and anointed Betty's body while quietly chanting and singing praises to the miraculous cycle of life and death.

The timing was perfect, and Harold felt sure that Betty had indeed planned her tea party with her passing in mind. Two days prior to her death, she had asked me, "How will I know when I'm really going to die?" I told her that I felt quite certain that, because she was a keenly intuitive person, she would "just know."

We finished the ritual bathing at a quarter past two, and at a quarter to three, guests began to arrive. Harold and a friend greeted people at the door and let them know that Betty was still the guest of honor at this gathering but that her spirit had left her body a little while before. Some were shocked to walk in and see Betty's lifeless body, but most of them were touched by her beauty and by how appropriate it was that she had gathered her friends together in the warmth of her sweet home to share love and stories one last time.

May the blessings of Life rest upon you.
May a peace abide in you. May love's presence illuminate
your heart, now and forever more.

—*Sufi chant*

REAL LIFE SUPPORT

Come away, oh human child
To the waters and the wild
With a faery, hand in hand,
For the world's more full of weeping than you can understand.

—*William Butler Yeats*, from the poem "The Stolen Child"

T aking a deep breath, allow your mind to focus on a place in your body where you are feeling some pain, some discomfort, right now. Notice any particular sensations that arise. In your mind's eye, if you can, allow an image to come to you as you reside in that place. It can be anything...a color, an object imagined or real...anything."

Kit lay on a green leather couch in the cozy office of the local Cancer Resource Center and participated in a guided imagery session. (Guided imagery is a method of pain and symptom management that offers a guided meditative experience and encourages the use of inner resources for self-healing.) Kit was a forty-eight-year-old, single mother of two young boys, eight and eleven. She had metastatic stomach cancer. Her younger child was autistic, and Kit had spent the past eight years learning to communicate with this special being. This was indeed a sad story. Letting go of someone who is so young and beautiful is always hard. Letting go when children are being left behind is even harder.

Inspirational art and posters covered the walls of the center. Kit breathed deeply and slowly, her thick blonde hair flowing onto the soft brown pillows. Each breath in, she went a bit deeper inside, letting go of external distractions. Sorting through her confusion, she asked, "What does it mean, to allow an image to come?" and then she began to cry. She waited for a while and then spoke again.

"The image is a slide," she tells me. "You know, the kind at the park when we were kids. You climb up a long metal ladder on one side, sit at the top contemplating your next moment with both excitement and fear, and then you let go and slide down the shiny metal sweep. My sister is there to catch me."

She became silent and I asked what was happening. She said that she didn't want to "go there," to see her sister. She felt her sister offering help, but she wasn't ready for that yet.

"Kit," I said, knowing that her sister had died years ago, at the age of thirty-nine, "your sister is there to catch you, to hold you, to support you in this entire process, not just when you're dying. Feeling your sister's presence today does not mean you are going to die tomorrow."

Kit inhaled, considered this thought, slowly exhaled and then continued going deeper. She described the slide in detail: "It is orange and yellow, and the railings are rusty in some places." She talked about the fun of letting go and sliding down. She pictured herself doing it numerous times and laughing and enjoying herself. Kit and I had discovered early on that we both loved water and so we agreed that it could even be a water slide, and at the bottom she would end up floating.

Kit kept this image alive for months.

❧

On a Tuesday afternoon in early June as I returned home from teaching a caregiver training class, I got a call from Darcy, Kit's friend and advocate at the Cancer Resource Center. I knew that Kit had spent the past week in a palliative care suite in a hospital in Santa Rosa. "They let Kit out of the hospital last night," she told me, her own voice cracking a bit. "She is on hospice now. She is scared, but she doesn't want to ask for assistance. We are having a meeting today of all who might be of help in her care. Can you come?"

I emptied and repacked my car and prepared to drive another sixty miles back over the hills of Mendocino County to meet with this team.

I walked into a circle of nine women and one man. It was a circle of people who loved Kit, who cared deeply about her and instinctively understood that it would take a group to share the daunting task of helping her in the dying process. This young woman had touched each of their hearts, and they were ready and willing to be of service in this last challenging phase of Kit's life. Most of the people in the circle had not walked this path before and certainly not with a peer, a friend and such a passionate young woman.

I spent that night at Kit's house. We stayed up late, having deep and complicated conversations. A week prior, I had asked Kit what she thought was happening inside her body. "This is going to take my life," she said. I then asked her what she wanted to happen. "A miracle," was her reply.

Tonight, what she wanted was hope and love and reassurance that everything would be all right. She also said clearly that she wanted enough pain medicine to keep her really comfortable, and enough anti-emetic to keep her from being nauseated and vomiting. This attitude was new. Kit had turned down Western medicines for months. She was afraid of using too much or of being too sleepy and out of control. Her opening to these medicines seemed like a sign that she was more willing to let go of control and more open to surrendering to the experience of dying.

> There are common fears and major misconceptions about pain medicine in our culture. The "war on drugs" has made people afraid to use pain medication, even for the right reasons at the right times. When narcotics are used to control pain, there is a different cellular reaction than when they are used to get high. An educational campaign about this fact is needed in our society, if we are to help people die without suffering.

> Pain increases anxiety and stress and causes tightening of muscles, stomachs and minds. It affects every bodily system, clouds sensations, and gives the feeling of being crazy and confused. Often, once pain is adequately controlled, and sometimes with high doses of narcotics, clarity and communication become possible once again.

After a short night's sleep I awakened to a dazzling summer day in the golden hills of California. "Kit, I need to be the tough guy now and ask you a couple of hard questions. You can hate me." She laughed, saying it was not possible for her to hate anyone and opened her arms to hug me. I continued, "We need to discuss this DNR form. I know we've talked about this many times, but now it's not just an idea, it's the real thing. The hospice needs you to sign the form so that you don't get readmitted to the hospital if somebody panics and calls 911. We need everyone to be on the same page here and understand what it is you want us to do. Resuscitation means bringing you back to life once your body has died. We need to know whether you want that or not. We all need to be clear about this, Kit, and we want to follow your instructions. "

She asked what would happen if the ambulance was called. I explained that if the paramedics showed up and she was not able to breathe or her heart had stopped, their protocol would be to perform CPR if there were no orders to the contrary. CPR would likely create an ugly event, because her tumors were all over her chest, abdomen, heart, lungs, esophagus and trachea. I told her she was much too fragile for them to pump on her chest without breaking a rib or causing some other trauma. I explained that she would likely end up on a ventilator, sedated and with IV medications dripping into her arm. Her friends would not be at her bedside round the clock, and her children could not come and go. The door would not be open to the sunshine and the singing birds. I knew from the many conversations with Kit and her support network at the Cancer Resource Center that living at home and dying at home were important to her. She lived in an intentional community where food, shelter, childcare, healthcare and education were taken care of. "We have discussed this before, Kit, and in the past you said you would not want resuscitation at the end. Is that still true?"

She turned to me with a sad and serious look and said, "That's right, I don't want to be resuscitated."

A few minutes passed. Then I looked at her. "Now will you sign the forms?"

"Give them to me," she laughed.

🙢

About a week later, Kit was riding big waves—her body was increasingly weaker but her spirit was strong and her own inner power was still palpable. There were days and hours when her pain was overwhelming and all that she wanted to do was sleep. Other days were okay—a few hours of pain and nausea and then several comfortable hours visiting with friends, her sons, and her ex-husband. Kit had not been connected to her ex-husband for years, so this was a particularly difficult time for them. She was not even certain who would care for her sons when she was gone. There were many poignant conversations, deep looks and long hugs. Kit and her loved ones spent time listening to music and doing a life review. They told stories about her past while a scrapbook of photos was assembled in the other room. Everyone who visited told Kit how much they loved her, and no one left the room without Kit's assurance that she loved and appreciated them. Gratitude flowed from her with the force of a wild river. Hospice nurses came and went. They spoke with the care team, adjusted the medicines, made phone calls to the pharmacy, helped Kit and her friends feel secure about the details of pain control, and offered their emotional support.

On a Monday evening, the caregiver circle reconvened. We talked about our feelings and our connections to Kit. The situation was getting more difficult. Various family and friends didn't understand the constant changes in medication protocols, so I explained the medical pieces of the puzzle. There was so much sadness in letting go of this exquisite young woman. We cried and cried. We talked and rescheduled our lives in order to be available round-the-clock. We offered solace to one another.

> It is crucial to support the caregivers. Those losing their loved ones need to be comforted and have their feelings heard. Unacknowledged grief becomes a festering wound. Compassionate listening is a healing salve.

After the meeting, some of us returned to Kit's sacred space and encircled her with healing prayers and songs. Then, for quite a while, we sat in silence and contemplation. After everyone left, Kit sat on the ottoman in front of my chair, and I massaged her back and neck. She needed to go through the conversation about the DNR one more time. "So," she said, "on my DNR form from a while ago, I wrote that I only wanted to be kept alive on a ventilator for a month. What do you think about that?"

I was taken aback. I wasn't sure what she was asking. She had signed the Pre-hospital Do Not Resuscitate form. Did she think she needed to write a different advance directive now that she was on hospice, or was she asking me again if she should go to the hospital and be put on a ventilator? I was confused.

Oddly enough, at the end of our caregivers meeting, someone had asked just this question: "What if she suddenly changes her mind when you are there, and says call 911...What do you do?" Stop and relax, we had all agreed, and talk with her. Find out what is going on inside. Is she afraid? Is she in more pain? Remind her that we *all* agreed not to call 911 and send her back to the hospital. Call hospice. Give her more morphine if she is in pain, per the hospice nurses' instructions. Call someone else on the team. We also agreed that if she insisted on it, we would call 911. As her caregivers, we were there to follow her lead, as long as she was coherent.

"Kit," I said to her directly, as I rubbed her back a bit more gently, "you are living in one of the most beautiful places on earth. You can feel the warmth of summer through the windows and fresh smells of ripening earth. You hear the animals, birds, children and music. If you go back to the hospital, you will end up in intensive care. You will have tubes in your throat and IV lines in your arms. A machine will push air into your lungs and make your chest rise and fall to mimic life. IV medications will make sure your heart is beating, but none of these things will return your quality of life. Western medicine and technology can prolong your state, that is true, but they will not cure your cancer or prevent you from dying. Your children and friends will only be allowed to visit you at certain times and hours. Consider this reality for a moment. Is this what you want?"

> What is called *life support* in a hospital is a ritual of technology that our culture has become dependent upon in our attempts to elude death. We have the capacity to escape mortality briefly. Certainly, this is one of the wonders of modern science. This ability is also one of the major downfalls, as proven by public cases like Nancy Cruzan, Robert Wendlin,

and Terri Schiavo—patients who were kept on life support, in persistent vegetative states, while the courts argued about their loved ones' rights to make decisions for them.

The wonder of the human spirit, in my own belief system, is that it continues on. Modern medicine defines death in terms of the lack of functioning of the brain, heart and lungs. I would define death as that moment when the spirit or breath or life force leaves the physical body it has inhabited. In our culture we tend to identify our personalities and spirits with a physical form. However, our bodies are not the totality of who we are. They are simply the vehicles that carry our spirits through this life. There will come a day for all of us when our bodies are left behind to decompose into the earth—just as shells are left on the sand. Hopefully, on that day, death will be understood as a sacred moment of transformation.

"Kit," I continued, "the friends and family gathered around you are your life support. We will hold you and massage your feet. We will turn you and bathe you and play the music you want to hear. We will help you sit up when you need to, and sip water or tea. We will love you unconditionally, listen to your fears, wipe your tears, and support your life until the very last moment—until your final in-breath and your final out-breath. *This* is real life support."

I sat with Kit for a while longer, and she asked more questions. She wanted to hear more about other deaths. I told her about my friend Kim, who lay dying in ICU, hooked up to every machine possible. I shared some of the lessons I had received about being a midwife to the dying and about the importance of expressing that it was all right to let go. (Although I have learned that this is not true for all cultures.) I explained that because of my own positive experiences with death, I was able to be present with her now. I shared memories about Helene, my sister, and the heart-opening process of her dying. I reminded Kit about her guided imagery work and the blessing of reuniting with her sister, Anne. Finally she sighed with relief. "OK," she whispered, "I'm tired now. And I'm sure that I don't want to go to the hospital. Please tell the others. Tell them not to call 911."

꧂

The following Friday was the day before the summer solstice. I had already told her friend Lynne and others that often people choose auspicious dates or times to die. I told them that I thought Kit might die on the solstice. So when the phone rang, I was not surprised.

"Things are changing," Darcy said. "Her breathing seems more difficult. She is less responsive. Can you come now?"

I had committed to being Kit's midwife, so I got in my car immediately and made one last journey across the mountains. Midwives at the deathbed do not catch the spirit, as midwives catch the child in birthing. We witness, guide and support the body and mind in order to serve the spirit by gently ushering it out of the confinement of the body. Because we are often not emotionally attached to the dying person and we are able to see things that have been overlooked, it is also our role to guide family and friends.

The ranch where Kit lived and died rests in a huge open peaceful valley, tucked between steep and wooded California hills. The long, narrow, winding road that leads from the highway to the ranch overlooks horses in their pastures and organic gardens bursting with food and flowers. The river in the distance flows among the tall fir and redwood trees and the shorter oaks. What an honor to witness the dying journey in such a special place.

I arrived to a house filled with the glow of summer sunset light, candles and soft music. I was hidden behind a large bouquet of white and yellow lilies, and even in her weakened and dreamy state, Kit smiled as the flowers entered the room before me.

Even though it was the solstice and the shortest night of the year, I could see that we were settling in for a sleepless one, once I saw Kit's shallow breathing and graying color.

"Has anyone told the boys to come and say goodbye?" I asked. Someone said, "Yes, I think so." There had been confusion around telling the children about their mother's dying. What was right? How should we tell them? I believe that children understand death. These boys knew that their mother was dying, and they also seemed to understand that it was time to reunite with their father, even though they had not seen him in many years.

The eleven-year-old, Ian, then came to the door. We asked Kit if she wanted some alone time and she nodded yes. A few minutes later we heard loud yelling and crying and hands banging on the rails of the hospital bed. "You're not going to die. Can't we take you to the doctor? No, no, no. You can't leave us." The crying and yelling and pain and anger went on for a while. Then it was quiet. Ian quickly left the house and ran across the road to the cabin where he was staying with his brother and father. The rest of us were silent and left Kit to the privacy of her tears.

A little while later, Ian came back and walked slowly and surely into the room—this time, right to his mother's side. "I'm OK now, Mom. When you die, I'll meet you out at our special tree in the woods, down by the creek, OK?"

"Okay," Kit smiled through her tears. "And when you think of me, you'll find a white feather on the ground."

It was the longest, shortest night of the year. Kit slowly slipped in and out of a coma; in and out of this world, and into the veils that I believe hold us between our reality and the unknown until we are absolutely ready to let go.

Each time Kit's breathing became more labored and her pain seemed to increase, she was given medicine to ease her discomfort and calm her anxiety. A small circle of women stayed awake all night—lay midwives to the dying. They had been drawn to do this work out of love for their friend and to honor something sacred and important. We sang quietly and touched her hands, head, and feet and assured her that she was loved, forgiven and appreciated. We assured her that the children would be cared for, as she had arranged. We told her that her love had opened our hearts.

Often the young take a longer time in the active dying phase. This is a period of time at the end of the dying process when breathing can become more labored and uneven. Sometimes the breathing stops and then resumes at a faster rate. Noises come from the throat, often called the *death rattle*. The heart rate can speed up or slow down dramatically. The feet, legs and hands may become cool and discolored, allowing the remaining blood and life force to be focused on the central core of the body. The moment of death draws near.

However, young hearts are normally strong, and energy can remain in the vital organs for a while. This was the case with Kit. The night sky began to lighten, and she was still with us. She was barely alive and did not speak or open her eyes any longer. Kit's shallow breathing remained a quiet erratic rhythm, rocking her soul to sleep.

Friends and family sometimes become anxious during this phase, especially when they have not witnessed a death before. How long can this go on? What can we do to help her? Can't we get more medicine? These are normal questions and fears. We are not accustomed to watching death reach its arms around our loved ones and carry them away. For some, dying is a very slow dance. Who knows what karma is being completed in those last moments, what lessons are being learned or what last bits of forgiveness the spirit must attend to?

"She is working hard," I reminded everyone gently. "She did not want to leave us. So it may take a while, even though it seems so close. She has her own work to do now, and we cannot interfere with that." I assured them that the medicines were working and that Kit was free from pain and suffering. By this time, her breathing was minimal, her heart was beating very slowly, and a look of peace radiated from her face. I called the hospice nurse and a doctor friend to allow Kit's loved ones to hear other reassuring voices confirm that she was simply taking her time and dying slowly.

As darkness lifted into the heavens, the first sun of summer rose over the top of the hills, illuminating sky and earth and trees and river. Surrounded by the loving circle of her *real life support* team, Kit died that solstice morning.

A week later, Ian walked around the ranch humming quietly and proudly carrying a large bouquet of white feathers.

Now is the time for the world to know
That every thought and action is sacred.

This is the time
For you to deeply compute the impossibility
That there is anything
But Grace.

Now is the season to know
That everything you do
Is sacred.

—*Hafiz*, from the poem "Now is the Time"

Part Four

PREPARING FOR THE FINAL CHAPTER OF LIFE

PLANNING FOR THE INEVITABLE

Learn about options
Implement a plan
Voice the plan to others
Engage others to live
It's About How You LIVE

These words are the motto of National Hospice and Palliative Care Organization (NHPCO). The goal of their campaign is to encourage people, regardless of their health status, to put end-of-life wishes in writing. For healthcare professionals, it is crucial to develop a depth of knowledge and understanding about creating meaningful advance directives for healthcare. Being comfortable in having difficult conversations with people, gracefully and compassionately, is a skill. It can be learned. There are resources and mentors available to assist in this learning process (see Resources). It is equally important, as human beings and as members of our society, for each of us to ask ourselves the formidable questions about end-of-life care and have conversations with friends, families, and even colleagues. No one is immune from disease and death. Life is, as the saying goes, sexually transmitted and terminal. As Sogyal Rinpoche (1993) tells us, "When we accept death, transform our attitude toward life, and discover the fundamental connection between life and death, a dramatic possibility for healing can occur."

The most important aspect of advance care planning is understanding what questions to ask and then discussing the answers with friends, family, and doctors. An advance directive (or Durable Medical Power of Attorney for Healthcare [DPOAH]) is meaningless without direct conversations with one's chosen agents about ideas, philosophies, fears and feelings about life and death, illness and suffering. During my years as an ICU nurse, there were numerous occasions when we would contact the agent listed on a patient's DPOAH and discover that they had no idea they had been named the person's agent and certainly had never had a conversation delineating the patient's wishes for end-of-life care.

In U.S. culture, we put a high premium on life. But life and death are both part of the big picture and to see one without the other is foolhardy. We are all going to die someday. Being prepared for that day provides security for loved ones and freedom for oneself.

If you were about to embark on a trip around the world, wouldn't you at least look at a map or a guidebook? Wouldn't you try to anticipate the weather in the countries you might be visiting so that you could be prepared with the proper clothing and equipment? Are you going backpacking or staying at hotels? Do you need shots, paperwork, visas, passports and money?

Death is the ultimate journey that each and every one of us will take. We can plan ahead for this journey with awareness and curiosity and use our innate wisdom to prepare for the unknown. In Buddhist cultures, individuals spend their lives preparing for the ultimate destination of death. In other cultures, contemplative practices and rituals are used to prepare for the inevitable end of life. Plato, when asked what was the most important thing to do in life, replied, "Practice dying."

We can practice dying through meditation or contemplation, or we can simply take time periodically to assess our fears and feelings and discuss this grand subject with our loved ones. Often it takes the death of someone close to us to get us thinking and talking about our own demise. Sometimes a news article, such as the story of Terri Schiavo, will cause thousands to finally complete their advance directive paperwork. When I give presentations to groups of healthcare professionals, there is always a large percentage of the audience that has not completed their directives, and having to raise their hands and admit this can sometimes be the catalyst that spurs action. Whatever the inspiration, seize the opportunity.

Advance directives for healthcare come in many forms. They can be simple or extremely detailed. They can be drawn up by lawyers or simply written in pen and witnessed by two observers.

It is important that clinicians be aware of the various types of directives available for their patients. POLST (Physician's Orders for Life Sustaining Treatment—see Resource section) forms are new to many healthcare systems and providers and are particularly useful for residents of facilities or those who are nearing the end of life but may not be on hospice as yet. These forms are physician orders that delineate specific wishes that have been agreed upon by doctor and patient.

Some questions about life and death to consider when completing an advance directive include:

- Did you grow up with a strong religious faith that informs your feelings about death?
- Do you believe that religion and spirituality are the same thing, and if not, how are they different?
- What has helped you most when you have lost someone close to you?
- Do you have friends or family who will be comfortable being at your bedside?

- Do you want to die at home, or does it matter?
- Who are the people you would most like to have at your bedside?
- Do you want music, a certain kind of lighting, quiet?
- What are your feelings about pain management?
- Can you have an honest conversation with your doctor?
- Do you want to write your own obituary? Do you want to orchestrate your own memorial service or funeral?
- Are there certain prayers, readings, poems or words that you wish to hear when you are dying?
- Are there rituals that you would like performed?
- Have you considered writing or recording an "Ethical Will"—a way to pass on your values and allow loved ones to know what was most important in your lifetime?

The ultimate gift to friends and family is being prepared for the end of life. When your dying time comes, it is important that your loved ones can spend quality time sitting with you, talking, praying, singing or just being quiet. When preparations have been made, phone calls or running around to doctors and mortuaries trying to guess what was wanted at the end of life can be avoided.

The Center for Bioethics (2010) says it this way:

We live within webs of social relationships—family, school, work, faith. We mark many of the predictable landmarks of our lives with social rituals—birthdays, graduations, weddings, retirements, and burials. However, social rituals that mark life's last chapter are uncommon. Without such rituals, the end of life in America is marked in other ways. Patients suffer in pain that could and should be managed. Seriously ill patients and their loved ones needlessly suffer spiritual, psychological, and social distress. Too often, the financial costs of caring for dying patients are catastrophic, but the benefits of the care are marginal. Preferences concerning care at the end of life are not expressed or heard, or they are heard but not respected. The value of life's last chapter may be missed entirely.

When we enter the field of healthcare, we accept responsibility to see our patients through times of stress, disease, healing, living and ultimately dying. We must find ways personally and professionally to help ensure that life's last chapter is not missed.

HOSPICE AND PALLIATIVE CARE

Providing Hope and Comfort at the End of Life

If you lose hope, somehow you lose the vitality that keeps life moving, you lose that courage to be, that quality that helps you go on
in spite of it all. And so today I still have a dream.
—*Dr. Martin Luther King, Jr.*

Changes in care at the end of life are not going to happen with
marginal adjustments in the way we organize services. It takes a
much more sustained effort on many fronts to refocus priorities for
the care of the critically ill. Changes in social norms, professional
values, and social priorities all need to be part of the solution.
—*Joanne Lynne*, MD, 1995

I am often shocked at most responses to the word *hospice*, even
within the healthcare community. It seems that hospice has
become synonymous with *death* and *morphine*. I often hear
that patients don't want to go on hospice for a multitude of reasons,
including these: they are not ready to "give up hope," they are not
ready to die, or they do not want to be "overdosed" with morphine.

Families do not want loved ones to "think they are dying." Physicians have been heard to express similar ideas with statements such as, "My patient is not at that stage yet."

Given recent statistics about hospice, these attitudes are not entirely surprising. The average length of stay in hospice in this country is twenty-one days, and thirty percent of hospice patients die in less than seven days. It is true that when patients are finally admitted to hospice care, it is most often at the very end of life, and they do need morphine and other medications to keep them comfortable. However, waiting until a crisis or collapse does not demonstrate a good model for compassionate care. If hospice was initiated six months prior to death:

- The dying patient would experience relief of ongoing suffering.
- Loved ones would receive regular counseling and access to needed resources.
- Healing relationships would be established over time
- Hospices would be more financially solvent.

One reason hospice is underutilized is because some doctors are reticent to make the referral. They too believe that a hospice referral means giving up or succumbing to the fact that they can no longer help or heal the patient. Doctors and nurses must understand how much healing occurs when patients and families have access to needed and deserved resources, are being communicated with honestly and directly, and are offered kindness and compassion in their last days, weeks or months of life.

If we want to establish a greater understanding and acceptance of hospice and palliative care, we must learn how to discuss the concepts in ways that emphasize quality of life and living, expert pain and symptom management, and relief of every level of suffering.

When I sit with a client and family and initiate the dreaded hospice conversation, I have to be extremely sensitive and tactful. It is important that professionals are comfortable discussing the issues that surround end-of-life care, which include fear, denial and misconceptions. We must also be able to offer the choices for quality care and then sit back and follow the lead of the patient. This is not easy. We want to help, to fix things, to manage the patient's pain. Yet some patients have agendas about their dying process, and we must work diligently to respect that.

Recently I was called to see a seventy-five-year-old woman, Edith, who had metastatic breast cancer seventeen years after her initial diagnosis. It had spread to her bones, lungs, liver and brain. She was frail and weak, but denied any pain. She smiled at everyone and when asked how she was doing, she always answered, "I'm fine." She was still undergoing daily radiation treatments for the bone metastases when we met, and she and her husband, Albert, believed that she might get stronger after radiation and be able to do more chemotherapy.

The morning I visited, I spoke with Albert for a long time before meeting Edith. In the middle of our conversation, he received a call from the oncology RN case manager, and I could tell from his side of the conversation that she was suggesting it might be time for hospice. There was no explanation of what that meant, just the words. When he hung up, I asked if she had discussed hospice, and he said, "Yes; what the hell is that?" I explained to him in depth what hospice care entailed. I also explained that if the oncology team was proposing a hospice referral, it meant that they felt there was no further treatment to cure the cancer, and comfort care was now the most humane option.

This was the first time that Albert understood that his wife was going to die. I discussed the fact that hospice requires a physician to state that if a disease progresses in an expected pattern, the patient likely has six months or less to live. It was hard to have this conversation, having just met this man for the first time. However, as tears welled up in his eyes, he looked at me and said, "Why hasn't anyone else been as direct with me as you are? I can deal with the truth. I can handle things much more easily if I know what is really happening."

We owe our patients and their loved ones honesty and clear explanations of what diagnoses and prognoses mean. Yes, there will be those who do not wish to know the course of their disease, and that too must be honored. But in my experience, most prefer the truth.

꒰꒱

Palliative care is a new phrase in our common language. It comes from the root "palliate"—to cover or cloak, or to improve conditions. Palliative care is about providing comfort, easing suffering, and assisting a patient and loved ones in achieving optimum quality of life, even in the face of death. Suffering does not solely exist on the physical plane. I believe, as I have stated earlier, that death is indeed a spiritual experience and not a medical event, and the suffering that accompanies death is often greatest in the emotional and spiritual realms. Letting go of this life, planet, loved ones, and love of life is not an easy task. We can learn to support each other in this final phase of life by practicing compassion and educating one another about choices and options for care.

The philosophy of hospice includes palliative care, but palliative care does not necessarily include or preclude hospice. One of the many misinterpretations of palliative care is that it is only for the dying. Palliative care serves people at any stage of illness. It can be a bridge between acute care and hospice, holistically addressing the suffering of an individual who can no longer be cured of a disease but who must be comforted.

In the palliative care program that I direct at JFCS in San Francisco, there are broad criteria that define our clients. We view the suffering of a young woman who is receiving weekly chemotherapy for a curable cancer as just as much a palliative care issue as the pain of a ninety-year-old with end-stage heart failure. We offer palliative care consultations, advocacy and volunteers to anyone in need.

A patient with end-stage disease should not be discharged from an acute hospitalization without at least an initial conversation about palliative and hospice care. Hopefully in the future, there will be a palliative care team, nurse, or social worker in every setting who is equipped to have this conversation and ensure that the level of care the patient needs at home will be manageable.

> So, I can't say I expected this to be such a life-affirming moment. But once my Dad got into Hospice and out of the hospital, and after he "got it" (that he was dying), it all just got quiet, and peaceful, and sort of lovely. That's a surprise. And a relief. It's been a really long month (and year.)
>
> —Excerpt from a letter from the daughter of a dying client

Those dying at home often need even more than hospice can provide. They need family and friends to serve as advocates and oversee the situation. Privately hired homecare may be required, which is not covered by insurance. If a strong support system does not exist at home, the dying loved one may need to be transferred to a facility or kept in the hospital. There is a growing need for residential hospice as well as palliative care suites in hospitals, venues where hope and healing can be maintained and dying can occur with peace and dignity.

Dr. Wendy S. Harpham (2007, *Oncology Times*) states in her column, "View from the Other Side of the Stethoscope,"

> Physicians who open the door to hope, help heal patients. What particular hope a patient might hold onto depends on what hope helps that patient live fully, especially at the end of life. Some patients find peace and happiness in their last

days by letting go of all hopes of recovery, instead hoping for comfort and loving kindness as they slip away. Others find happiness by preparing for death, and then, until their dying breath, holding tight to their comforting hopes for a cure…Expectation is a state of mind; hope is a state of heart. Doctors and nurses help patients heal when we separate our hopes from our expectations, and then share both with our patients. By guiding patients' efforts to deal with what is happening while encouraging them to nourish hope, we help people live until they die. (p. 33)

Whether we meet our patients at diagnosis, during treatment, over the course of a chronic illness, or at the end of life, this is the essence of our jobs as healthcare professionals: to nourish hope, to serve with compassion, and to help people live until they die. It is also the essence of our jobs as fellow citizens on this planet.

This existence of ours is as transient as autumn clouds.
To watch the birth and death of beings is like looking
at the movements of a dance.
A lifetime is like a flash of lightning in the sky,
Rushing by, like a torrent down a steep mountain.
—*The Buddha*

May all beings be free from suffering.
May all beings live and die in peace.

EPILOGUE

Job Description
For Any Member of a Palliative Care Team
(For Elliot)

I am here to witness
the sacred hearts
broken open
Friends, lovers, families
whose loved ones die in their arms
In their homes, in their beds, in hospitals or other places
Peacefully, or not

I am here to witness
the sanctity of human life
As the spirit is released from the temple
to join once again, with the invisible cellular infinity
of the Universe
the mitochondria of the Milky-Way
Becoming energy to light the stars
since we know—
the energy we manifest as a particular human being

like any other,
can neither be created
nor destroyed
God by any other name, by any name, by many names, by no name
Is
One

I am here to witness
the breath
as it enters the body
and exits for the last time
The miracle of birth
The miracle of death
The miracle of each moment in between:
Life
The infusion of consciousness
into each and every cell
enduring every moment
we are here
on earth

I am here to witness
To feel
To experience
To honor
To know that Love is eternal
To share
this blessing
in gratitude

and to perform any other duties
required

ACKNOWLEDGMENTS

As with most things in life, we do not accomplish our goals alone. I have many people to thank for helping birth this book. I thank Julie Rumble, for encouraging me to keep a journal of the hospital stories that she listened to me recount, week after week, year after year. I also thank her for giving me the title of this book during a phone conversation when she said, "Redwing, what you offer people is the last act of kindness."

I thank my brother, Alex Keyssar, for coming closer and closer as we lost the others of our immediate family and for reminding me that writing a book is tiring, frustrating, and worth it. He knows; he has written several.

My dear friend Danielle Shapona believed in me and in this project, understood the depths of the work, shared moments at deathbeds with me, offered Reiki to the dying (as well as to me), and took photos for the cover. My heartfelt gratitude goes out to you.

To my teachers, Sharon Hunter, Marcia Weeks, Joan Halifax, Deena Metzger, Ruth Dennison, Evelyn Eaton; my colleagues at Mendocino Coast District Hospital, where I built my foundation in nursing skills; to Zomala Abell and Maggie Watson, for co-creating our nonprofit, Transformations, to educate people about end-of-life care—a huge bow of gratitude. Special thanks to Jami Sieber, for bringing music into my workshops and for being a solid and supportive friend who also understands the energy required to produce a work of art. Thanks to Judy Lynch for being the kind of boss everyone wishes they had, and to Gwen Harris and Eric Poche for sharing my passion for this work, on a day-to-day basis. To my team and community at JFCS, and to the SMS at UCSF, thank you.

The nitty-gritty of writing a book and publishing it could not have been accomplished without the help of editors Sarah Underhill and Marilyn Power Scott, my readers Pat Chiota, Betty Carmack and Terry Hill, book designer Dorothy Carico Smith, editor and book agent Amy Rennert. Thanks to Roberta Achtenberg for understanding the need for this book and introducing me to Amy.

The list of those who have died but never left my heart and mind is too long. I thank each and every one of them for their vulnerability, their trust, and the gifts they gave me in their dying. I especially thank Kim, Jo, Flame, Allison, Shelli, Lani, and Alicia. May their memories be a blessing.

GLOSSARY OF TERMS

A.N.D.: Acronym for "Allow Natural Death." An order to Allow Natural Death is meant to ensure that only comfort measures are provided. By using the AND, physicians and other medical professionals would be acknowledging that the person is dying and that everything that is being done for the patient—including the withdrawal of nutrition and hydration—will allow the dying process to occur as comfortably as possible.

Anesthetized: The condition of having sensation (including the feeling of pain) blocked or temporarily taken away. This allows patients to undergo surgery and other procedures without the distress and pain they would otherwise experience.

Brain death: Irreversible cessation of all functions of the entire brain, including the brain stem.

Caloric Testing for Brain death: A routine test for determining brain death which involves the injection of 50-cc ice water into the external auditory canal. When the brain stem is functioning this will cause an automatic response of both eyes deviating toward the irrigated ear. Both sides need to be tested with an interval of five minutes.

CCU: Coronary care units, give intensive medical care to patients with severe heart disease.

Chemical Restraints: Medication used to control behavior or restrict the patient's freedom of movement. Generally used as an alternative to physical restraints.

Do-Not-Resuscitate (DNR) Orders: Instructions written by a doctor telling other healthcare providers not to try to restart a patient's heart, using cardiopulmonary resuscitation (CPR) or other related treatments, if his/her heart stops beating. Usually, DNR orders are written after a discussion between a doctor and the patient and/or family members. DNR orders are written for people who are very unlikely to have a successful result from CPR—those who are terminally ill or those who are elderly and frail.

Electrolyte: A substance that will dissociate into ions in solution and acquire the capacity to conduct electricity. The electrolytes include sodium, potassium, chloride, calcium and phosphate.

Extubation: The process of removing a tube from a hollow organ or passageway, often from the airway.

Feeding tube: A medical device used to provide nutrition to patients who cannot obtain nutrition by swallowing. The state of being fed by a feeding tube is called enteral feeding or tube feeding. Placement may be temporary for the treatment of acute conditions or lifelong in the case of chronic disabilities. A variety of feeding tubes are used in medical practice.

Gastric feeding tube (G-tube): A feeding tube inserted through a small incision in the abdomen into the stomach and is used for long-term enteral nutrition.

Glioblastoma: Glioblastoma multiforme (GBM) is the most common and most aggressive type of primary brain tumor in humans.

ICU: The intensive care unit has special equipment and staff to care for very ill patients.

Intubation: The process of putting a tube into a hollow organ or passageway, often into the airway. The opposite of intubation is extubation.

Malignancy: A tumor that is malignant, that is cancerous, that can invade and destroy nearby tissue, and that may spread (metastasize) to other parts of the body.

Metastases: The cancer resulting from the spread of the primary tumor. For example, someone with melanoma may have a metastasis in his or her brain. And a person with colon cancer may, fortunately, show no metastases. Metastasis depends on the cancer cells acquiring two separate abilities—increased motility and invasiveness. Cells that metastasize are basically of the same kind as those in the original tumor. If a cancer arises in the lung and metastasizes to the liver, the cancer cells in the liver are lung cancer cells. However, the cells have acquired increased motility and the ability to invade another organ.

Nasogastric feeding tube (NG-tube): A feeding tube passed through the nares, down the esophagus and into the stomach.

Orthostatic hypotension: A rapid drop in blood pressure that occurs when a person sits up or stands up from a sitting or lying position. This can cause dizziness or possibly fainting.

Resuscitation: The procedure of restoring to life, as in cardiopulmonary resuscitation (CPR).

Terminal Agitation: a restlessness which maybe experienced in the end-phase of a terminal illness.

Terminal sedation: (also known as **palliative sedation**) is the practice of relieving distress in a terminally ill person in the last hours or days of a patient's life, usually by means of a continuous intravenous or subcutaneous infusion of a sedative drug.

Ventilator: Also known as a respirator, is a machine that pushes air into the lungs through a tube placed in the trachea (breathing tube). Ventilators are used when a person cannot breathe on his or her own or cannot breathe effectively enough to provide adequate oxygen to the cells of the body or rid the body of carbon dioxide.

RESOURCES

Coalition for Compassionate Care of California
http://finalchoices.org/
The Coalition for Compassionate Care of California is a partnership of more than ninety-five regional and statewide organizations dedicated to the advancement of palliative medicine and end-of-life care in California. Their site contains information on research and public policy, guidelines for planning advanced care, and a link to download the California POLST (Physician Orders for Life-Sustaining Treatment) form.

California Culture Change Coalition
www.calculturechange.org
This site provides information on the movement to fundamentally change the way nursing homes operate. *Culture change* in this context refers to care that focuses on people and relationships. The site provides education and resources on this concept and includes links to national resources as well as partners in other states.

California Medical Association—Advance Directives FAQ and Resources
www.cmanet.org/publicdoc.cfm?docid=7&parentid=4

This resource provides answers to most commonly asked questions on advance directives. An *Advance Health Care Directive Kit* is available for purchase through the online bookstore.

CancerPEN
ecampus.stanford.edu/
The Stanford Cancer Palliation Education Network (CancerPEN) is a web-based palliative care national learning community. This is an excellent resource for learning how to have difficult conversations with patients and families.

Caring Connections
www.caringinfo.org/
A program of the National Hospice and Palliative Care Organization, this is a community engagement initiative to improve care at the end of life. The site provides downloads of state-specific advance directives and a guide to planning end-of-life care.

Center to Advance Palliative Care (CAPC)
www.capc.org/
CAPC is a national organization dedicated to increasing the availability of quality palliative care services for those facing serious illness. It provides healthcare professionals with the tools, training and technical assistance necessary to start and sustain successful palliative care programs in hospitals and other health care settings. Direction and technical assistance are provided by Mount Sinai School of Medicine.

Eden Alternative
www.edenalt.org/
The Eden Alternative is a small nonprofit organization making a big difference in the world. The organization's core belief is that aging

should be a continued stage of development and growth rather than a period of decline.

FINAL PASSAGES
www.finalpassages.org/
Final Passages is a model project offering education for personal and legal rights concerning home or family-directed funerals and final disposition (burial and cremation). Its intention is to reintroduce the concept of funerals in the home as a part of family life and as a way to deinstitutionalize death. It is dedicated to a dignified and compassionate alternative to current funeral practices. A resource book is available for sale through the web site.

A GRACEFUL FAREWELL
This comprehensive soft-cover book by Maggie Watson offers clear, user-friendly, step-by-step guidance in getting one's affairs in order. Its tear-out, three-hole-punched, fill-in-the-blanks pages cover a multitude of areas, including personal and family information, legal matters and final wishes. It is available from Cypress House: **www.cypresshouse.com.**

JEWISH FAMILY AND CHILDREN'S SERVICES (JFCS) OF THE SAN FRANCISCO BAY AREA
www.jfcs.org/
Since 1850, JFCS has provided comprehensive social services to Bay Area residents of all ages and faiths. It helps solve personal problems—from cradle to rocking chair—in order to strengthen the individual, the family, and the community.

LONG TERM CARE INSURANCE NATIONAL ADVISORY CENTER
www.longtermcareinsurance.org/
This organization is dedicated to helping evaluate and compare

various long-term care insurance policies. They provide answers to common questions and develop a comparison of policies and prices based on each client's information.

NATIONAL HOSPICE AND PALLIATIVE CARE ORGANIZATION—NHPCO
www.nhpco.org/templates/1/homepage.cfm
This is the largest nonprofit membership organization representing hospice and palliative care programs and professionals in the United States. The organization is committed to improving end-of-life care and expanding access to hospice care. The site includes links to research, resources, care providers, breaking news in the field, and education opportunities.

PHYSICIAN ORDERS FOR LIFE-SUSTAINING TREATMENT
(POLST) PARADIGM PROGRAM
www.polst.org/
The POLST mission is to facilitate POLST paradigm programs in every state. It also provides information on each state's current status with regard to the POLST paradigm. In addition, legal and community resources as well as a guide to implementing a POLST program can be found.

POLST BROCHURE FROM THE
CALIFORNIA COALITION FOR COMPASSIONATE CARE
http://www.finalchoices.org/polst.php#brochure
This site provides simple and easy-to-read information about POLST and a glossary of some medical terms discussed in end-of-life care.

PUT IT IN WRITING
www.putitinwriting.org/putitinwriting_app/index.jsp
This simple and accessible web brochure was created by the American Hospital Association. It offers information about advance

directives as well as links to worksheets, tool kits, and sites with legal information.

Respecting Choices
www.respectingchoices.org/
This site is home of the Gundersen Lutheran's Respecting Choices Organization & Community Advance Care Planning Course. This group offers a comprehensive curriculum which has become the model for end-of-life care in many states across the U.S. and internationally. The site has links to a research library and offers various course materials and consultations.

Sacred Dying Project
www.sacreddying.org/
The Sacred Dying Foundation is dedicated to challenging the way our society experiences death and dying. The Foundation's primary goal is to return the sacred to the act of dying by serving those who are at the end of life.

Seniors At Home
www.seniorsathome.org/
Seniors At Home is the senior services division of Jewish Family and Children's Services of San Francisco, the Peninsula, Marin and Sonoma Counties. Seniors At Home houses a unique community-based Palliative and End-of-Life Care Program, and has created a process for the transition involving caring for the dying at home.

Threshold Choir
www.thresholdchoir.org/
The all-women Threshold Choir honors the ancient tradition of singing at the bedsides of those who are struggling—some with living, some with dying. The voice, as the original human instrument, is a

true and gracious vehicle for compassion and comfort. The choirs exist all over the United States and in several other countries and provide opportunities for women to share the sacred gift of voice at life's threshold.

Upaya Institute and Zen Center
www.upaya.org/
Upaya Zen Center is a residential Buddhist community located in Santa Fe, New Mexico. As a Zen center, daily meditation is open to the public. Other offerings include weekly public Dharma talks, which often highlight Buddhist teachings; a residential Path of Service and work exchange program; and weekly retreats and workshops that focus on practices related to engaged Buddhism and how to live in the world responsibly, with affection, kindness, and wisdom. Roshi Joan Halifax is the director of Upaya and teaches a yearly in-depth course for healthcare professionals called "Being With Dying."

Zen Hospice Project
www.zenhospice.org/
Inspired by a 2,500 year-old-tradition, Zen Hospice Project aims at cultivating wisdom and compassion through service. They provide a spectrum of collaborative services in end-of-life care, including residential hospice care, volunteer programs and public education events, which support mutually beneficial relationships among caregivers and individuals facing death.

BIBLIOGRAPHY

Jeanne Achterberg. *Woman as Healer.*
Boston, Shambala Publications, 1991.

Angeles Arrien. *The Four-Fold Way.* New York, Harper, 1993.

Sylvia Boorstein. *Don't Just Do Something, Sit There!*
San Francisco, Harper, 1996.

Ira Byock. *The Four Things That Matter Most.*
New York, Free Press, 2004.

Center for Practical Bioethics. *Caring Conversations,* workbook.
Author, rev. 2010. Available from www.practicalbioethics.org

Ram Dass. *Be Here Now.*
New York, Three Rivers Press, 1971.

Wendy S. Harpham. "The Risk of Hope," *Oncology Times* 29:9
(2007, May 10): 33

Michael Kearney. *Mortally Wounded.*
New York, Scribner, 1996.

Joanne Lynne. "Study to Understand Prognoses and Preferences for
Outcomes and Risks of Treatments," *JAMA,* (1995, November 22).

Wayne Muller. *How Then, Shall We Live?*
New York, Bantam, 1997.

Rachel Naomi Remen. *Kitchen Table Wisdom.*
New York, Riverhead, 1997.

Sogyal Rinpoche. *The Tibetan Book of Living and Dying.*
New York, HarperCollins, 1993.

Cappy Capossela and Sheila Warnock. *Share the Care: How to Organize a Group to Care for Someone Who Is Seriously Ill.*
New York, Share the Caring, Inc. Available through www.sharethecare.org.

ABOUT THE AUTHOR

Judith Redwing Keyssar, RN, BA, is the Director of the Palliative and End-of-Life Care Program at Seniors at Home, a division of Jewish Family and Children's Services (JFCS) of the San Francisco Bay Area. Previously, she was the Director of Patient Care Services for Zen Hospice Project (ZHP). Ms. Keyssar also spent fifteen years working in intensive care, oncology and hospice.

As a leader and innovator in the field of palliative care, she has given presentations to professional audiences across the country. Through her own nonprofit program, Transformations in Care, as well as through ZHP and JFCS, she has taught volunteers and family caregivers from eighteen years old to ninety years old. She has served hundreds of patients and families as they have experienced the last sacred moments of life.

Ms. Keyssar is also an artist, songwriter, and poet. One of her goals is to put healing back into healthcare. She looks forward to the day when death is again widely understood as a part of life.

For more information, see www.lastactsofkindness.com